Kindergarten Teacher's Guide

NATIONAL GEOGRAPHIC LEARNING | CENGAGE Learning

Exploring Science

Focus on the NEXT GENERATION SCIENCE STANDARDS For States, By States*

Program Authors

Randy L. Bell, Ph.D.
Malcolm B. Butler, Ph.D.
Kathy Cabe Trundle, Ph.D.
Judith S. Lederman, Ph.D.

Program Consultants

Gina Cervetti, Ph.D.
Nell K. Duke, Ed.D.
Philip E. Molebash, Ph.D.

Contents

Physical Science

Pushes and Pulls

Contents

Life Science

Contents

Earth Science

NOTES

Master the Next Generation Science Standards

Exploring Science provides expert instruction for the Next Generation Science Standards (NGSS). Implement the NGSS with confidence and ensure that your students master 21st century science skills. Combine instruction in Science and Engineering Practices, Disciplinary Core Ideas, and Crosscutting Concepts to meet the rigor of the Performance Expectations within the NGSS.

- Focus on 100% of the NGSS for grades K–5
- Introduce real-world science research with National Geographic Explorers, scientists, and photographers
- Connect NGSS content with investigations, engineering practices, and case studies for complete NGSS immersion

Grade K

Grade 1

Grade 2

Engage with print or eBook formats; both are available in English and Spanish to meet dual language needs.

Exploring Science for Kindergarten has three Big Books for Life, Earth, and Physical Science for whole class instruction of 100% of the NGSS. For grades 1-5, target 100% of the NGSS for Life, Earth, Physical Science, and Engineering Practices in one student book.

Grade 3

Grade 4

Grade 5

Student Support

Students receive all of the resources needed to gain a thorough understanding of NGSS concepts and practices. National Geographic visuals and engaging content capture student interest while reinforcing their understanding of the NGSS.

Print books and eBooks are available in English and Spanish.

Grade 2 Student Book

Support Disciplinary Core Ideas and Meet Performance Expectations

Hands-on activities provide support for Disciplinary Core Ideas and Performance Expectations within the NGSS. Investigate and Science in a Snap features offer opportunities for hands-on experiences to reinforce science concepts.

In the program, students are introduced to National Geographic Explorers and scientists who solve real-world problems. In Think Like a Scientist and Think Like an Engineer features, students meet Performance Expectations in ways such as making observations, designing solutions, planning and conducting investigations, making and using models, analyzing and interpreting data, and constructing arguments.

Teacher Support

Disciplinary Core Ideas and Performance Expectations are addressed thoroughly and concisely within the student books. The standard being taught is displayed on the page for clarity and simplicity

Teacher's Guides for each grade provide the support needed to implement and assess the NGSS. Master the NGSS Performance Expectations with lessons that are based on the 5E model of Engage, Explore, Explain, Elaborate and Evaluate.

Student Science Notebook opportunities

Grade 1 Teacher's Guide

NGSS and Objectives

Blocking Some Light

NEXT GENERATION SCIENCE STANDARDS | DISCIPLINARY CORE IDEAS

PS4.B: Electromagnetic Radiation Some materials allow light to pass through them, others allow only some light through and others block all the light and create a dark shadow on any surface beyond them, where the light cannot reach. [(Boundary: The idea that light travels from place to place is developed through experiences with light sources, mirrors, and shadows, but no attempt is made to discuss the speed of light.)] (1-PS4-3)

Objective **Students will be able to:**

- Describe materials that allow only some light to pass through them.

ENGAGE

Tap Prior Knowledge

- Ask: **What does it mean to say that a material or object is clear?** (*Clear* means that the material or object doesn't block any light.) **Can you see through a clear material?** (Yes.) **What do you think it would be like to look through a material that blocks *a little* light?** (Accept all student answers at this time.)

EXPLORE

Preview the Lesson

- Have students observe the image on pages 24–25. Ask: **What do you think this lesson is about?** (Some students may say they think the lesson is about butterflies, or the wings of the butterfly.)

Set a Purpose and Read

- Have students read in order to find out what happens when a material blocks only a little light.
- Read pages 24–25 together.

EXPLAIN

Describe Materials That Block Some Light

- Reread the paragraph on page 24 together. Ask: **What is the main topic of this lesson?** If students have trouble identifying the main topic, ask: **What is the one main thing that this lesson is trying to say?** (Some materials block a little light.) Have students point to the main topic.
- Ask: **What does an object look like when viewed through a material that lets only some light pass through it?** (Possible answers: It looks blurry. It is not very clear.) **How do you know?** (Possible answer: I know from the example in the text.) Have students point to the part of the text that helped them answer that question. (This butterfly's wings let some light through. You can see through them, but not very clearly.)
- Ask: **What part of the photo shows the main topic?** (the wing of the butterfly) **How does it show the main topic?** (You can sort of see the leaf through the wing, but it looks blurry.) Some students may have trouble seeing the difference between the blurriness of the image through the butterfly's wings and the blurriness of the rest of the background image that is a result of being out of focus. Have students use the more focused leaf in the lower left of the photo for comparison, rather than the background in the upper right.
- Ask students if they have ever looked through a foggy window. Ask: **Can you see through a foggy window?** (yes, but not very well) **Does a foggy window allow light to pass through it?** (only some light) **Which allows more light to pass through, a foggy window, or a clean window?** (a clean window)

5E Model

ELABORATE

Extend Your Thinking About Materials That Block Some Light

- Have students consider other examples of materials that block some light and ask them to make a list of them in their science notebook. Ask: **What are some other materials that allow just some light to pass through?** If students need help, say: **Think of materials that make things look blurry when you look through them.** (Possible answers: stained glass, frosted glass, waxed paper, apple juice, some plastic containers, colored cellophane, sunglasses)

Research How Sunglasses Work

- Help small groups of students do research to find out about an example of an object that blocks only some light—sunglasses. Have students look for answers to questions such as: **What types of light do sunglasses usually block? What is the purpose of blocking only some light? Why does some light need to pass through sunglasses? Are all sunglasses the same?** Remind students to write their findings in their science notebook.

EVALUATE

Have students record their answers to the Wrap It Up questions in their science notebook.

Wrap It Up!

1. RECALL **Why does the leaf look blurry through the butterfly's wings?** (The butterfly's wing blocks some light from passing through it.)
2. IDENTIFY **Name three things at home or school that block some light.** (Possible answers: colored plastic, foggy window, curtains)

ELL SUPPORT

Describe How Light Interacts With Materials

Beginning Ask yes/no questions to help students describe how light interacts with materials. For example: **Do some materials block a little light? Can you see through materials that block a little light?**

Intermediate Use sentence frames to help students describe how light interacts with materials. For example: *When materials block (some) of the light, you can see through them, but not (clearly).*

Advanced Provide sentence stems to help students describe how light interacts with materials. For example:

- *Clear materials…*
- *Materials that block some light…*

READING CONNECTION

Describe the Connection Between Ideas

Describe the connection between two individuals, events, ideas, or pieces of information in a text.

Guide students to describe the connection between two ideas in the text. For example, in the EXPLAIN section when asking students to compare a foggy window and a clean window, you might want to first explicitly relate this lesson to the previous one. Ask: **How does the main topic of this lesson relate to the main topic of the lesson on pages 22–23?** (This lesson is about materials that block some light, and the previous lesson was about materials that block no light.) After establishing this connection, probe to find out if any students can predict the next lesson before they turn the page.

PHYSICAL SCIENCE Waves: Light and Sound

Various Kinds of Lesson Supports for:

- Reading Connection
- Differentiated Instruction
- ELL Support
- Science Background
- Teach with Technology

Physical Science

Grade K. Forces and Interactions: Pushes and Pulls

Performance Expectations

Students who demonstrate understanding can:

K-PS2-1. Plan and conduct an investigation to compare the effects of different strengths or different directions of pushes and pulls on the motion of an object. [Clarification Statement: Examples of pushes or pulls could include a string attached to an object being pulled, a person pushing an object, a person stopping a rolling ball, and two objects colliding and pushing on each other.] [*Assessment Boundary: Assessment is limited to different relative strengths or different directions, but not both at the same time. Assessment does not include non-contact pushes or pulls such as those produced by magnets.*]

K-PS2-2. Analyze data to determine if a design solution works as intended to change the speed or direction of an object with a push or a pull. [Clarification Statement: Examples of problems requiring a solution could include having a marble or other object move a certain distance, follow a particular path, and knock down other objects. Examples of solutions could include tools such as a ramp to increase the speed of the object and a structure that would cause an object such as a marble or ball to turn.] [*Assessment Boundary: Assessment does not include friction as a mechanism for change in speed.*]

Disciplinary Core Ideas

PS2.A: Forces and Motion

- Pushes and pulls can have different strengths and directions. (K-PS2-1), (K-PS2-2)
- Pushing or pulling on an object can change the speed or direction of its motion and can start or stop it. (K-PS2-1), (K-PS2-2)

PS2.B: Types of Interactions

- When objects touch or collide, they push on one another and can change motion. (K-PS2-1)

PS3.C: Relationship Between Energy and Forces

- A bigger push or pull makes things speed up or slow down more quickly. *(secondary to K-PS2-1)*

ETS1.A: Defining Engineering Problems

- A situation that people want to change or create can be approached as a problem to be solved through engineering. Such problems may have many acceptable solutions. *(secondary to K-PS2-2)*

Science and Engineering Practices

Planning and Carrying Out Investigations

Planning and carrying out investigations to answer questions or test solutions to problems in K–2 builds on prior experiences and progresses to simple investigations, based on fair tests, which provide data to support explanations or design solutions.

- With guidance, plan and conduct an investigation in collaboration with peers. (K-PS2-1)

Analyzing and Interpreting Data

Analyzing data in K–2 builds on prior experiences and progresses to collecting, recording, and sharing observations.

- Analyze data from tests of an object or tool to determine if it works as intended. (K-PS2-2)

Connections to Nature of Science

Scientific Investigations Use a Variety of Methods

- Scientists use different ways to study the world. (K-PS2-1)

Crosscutting Concepts

Cause and Effect

- Simple tests can be designed to gather evidence to support or refute student ideas about causes. (K-PS2-1), (K-PS2-2)

K-2-ETS1 Engineering Design

ETS1-1. Ask questions, make observations, and gather information about a situation people want to change to define a simple problem that can be solved through the development of a new or improved object or tool.

Disciplinary Core Ideas

ETS1.A: Defining and Delimiting Engineering Problems

- A situation that people want to change or create can be approached as a problem to be solved through engineering. (K-2-ETS1-1)
- Asking questions, making observations, and gathering information are helpful in thinking about problems. (K-2-ETS1-1)

Science and Engineering Practices

Asking Questions and Defining Problems

Asking questions and defining problems in K–2 builds on prior experiences and progresses to simple descriptive questions.

- Ask questions based on observations to find more information about the natural and/or designed world(s). (K-2-ETS1-1)
- Define a simple problem that can be solved through the development of a new or improved object or tool. (K-2-ETS1-1)

How Things Move

NEXT GENERATION SCIENCE STANDARDS | DISCIPLINARY CORE IDEAS

PS2.A: Forces and Motion Pushing or pulling on an object can change the speed or direction of its motion and can start or stop it. (K-PS2-1), (K-PS2-2)

Objectives **Students will be able to:**

- Explain that things can move, and that when they do, they are in motion.
- Identify various types of motion.

Science Vocabulary
motion

ENGAGE

Tap Prior Knowledge

- Have students think about a game or a sport that they have participated in or watched. Then have students describe the movements that occur during the game. For example, during a baseball game, a batter swings a bat to hit the ball into the air. While swimming, a swimmer kicks his or her legs up and down in the water. Encourage volunteers to act out one of these movements. Then have the class describe the action.

EXPLORE

Preview the Lesson

- Display pages 4–5. Have students share what they see in the scene with the children jumping rope. Direct students to notice what is moving in the picture. Ask: **What are the children doing? What do you think the girl is doing between the ropes?** Have students share their ideas with the class. Invite children to share if they have ever jumped rope, and if they did, how they moved.

Set a Purpose and Read

- Have a volunteer point out the bold term *motion* on page 4. Read the main heading, and then ask: **How do you think the main heading "How Things Move" relates to the word *motion*? Think about this question as you listen to find out about how things move.**
- Have students follow along as you read aloud pages 4–5.

EXPLAIN

Define Motion

- Reread the heading and text on page 4, pointing to the word *motion* when it is read. Point to the girl jumping rope and say: **The girl is moving up and down. She is in *motion*.** Explain that there are different kinds of motions, such as up and down, back and forth, and round and round.
- Point to different things in the pictures on pages 4–5, asking students to identify whether the object or person might be in motion. Encourage students to use descriptive language to explain how the person or object might be moving. For example, point to the bicycle and ask: **Is this bicycle in motion?** (Yes.) **How do you know?** (Possible answer: The man looks like he is moving his legs to pedal the bike; his pedaling looks like it is making the wheels spin around; spinning wheels would move the bike forward.)

Describe How Things Move

- Point to the picture of the girl jumping rope and read the caption aloud. Say: **The girl is jumping up in the air. She is jumping between the two ropes. What do you think happened just after the picture was taken?** (Possible answer: The girl moved back down to the ground.) Invite students to jump up and down to imitate the movements of the girl jumping rope.
- Say: **The girl jumps up and down.** Ask: **What else is moving in this picture?** (the ropes) **What is causing the ropes to move?** (Possible answer: Children are holding the ends of the ropes on either side, and are swinging them around in circles as the girl jumps over them.) **How could the children make the ropes stop moving?** (They could stop swinging the ropes.)
- Point to the picture on page 5 of the man riding the bicycle. Explain that round things, such as wheels, can easily roll when put in motion. This is why round wheels are used on objects that people want to put in motion, such as bicycles, cars, and trucks.

- Ask: **Do you think the bicycle is moving quickly or slowly?** (probably quickly) **What might make the bicycle move this way?** (Possible answer: The man riding the bicycle looks like he is pedaling very hard and fast. This would make the bicycle move quickly.) **How could the man make his bicycle stop moving?** (He could stop pedaling and let it coast. He could also use the brakes to slow down and stop the bike.)

ELABORATE

Find Out More About Motion

My science notebook **Step 1:** Have students work in small groups to find pictures of things that look like they are in motion. Provide illustrated books or Internet resources for students to explore. Encourage groups to think of what might be causing the people or objects in their picture to move. Have students write a sentence in their science notebook to explain each type of motion shown in their pictures. **Step 2:** If time permits, invite groups to share their pictures with the class, explaining the type of motion being shown.

Extend Your Thinking About Moving Up and Down

My science notebook Say: **I throw a ball up in the air.** Ask: **What will happen?** (The ball will fall back down.) If possible, show children this motion by tossing a ball or a sheet of crumpled paper in the air and allowing it to fall to the ground. Generate a discussion with students about why the ball came back down. Explain that things fall because of Earth's gravity, which is a force that pulls everything on Earth toward the center of the planet. When throwing a ball up in the air, you actually have to provide a force greater than gravity to make the ball travel up. Invite students to draw a picture of something that can move up and down (jumping person, a bouncing basketball, seesaw) in their science notebook.

EVALUATE

My science notebook Have students record their answer to the Wrap It Up question in their science notebook.

Wrap It Up!

1. **RECALL Name two ways that things can move.** (Possible answers: up and down; round and round)

ELL SUPPORT

How Do Things Move?

Beginning Have students sort pictures of items that are moving and are not moving. Ask either/or questions about the type of movement. *(Is the boat walking or sailing?)*

Intermediate Help students identify the name of the person or object that is moving and the type of movement shown in the pictures they found. Provide sentence frames, such as: *The ________ walks up the hill. The cat ________ on the box.*

Advanced Encourage students to use descriptive words when writing sentences about the pictures they found. For example, they might write, *The cat jumps on the box.* Have them look at the picture and think of a way to describe the movement.

READING CONNECTION

Understand Unknown Words

With prompting and support, ask and answer questions about unknown words in a text.

Guide students to ask and answer questions about unknown words in a text. For example, in the EXPLORE section as you preview the text with students and set a purpose for reading, have a volunteer point out the bold term *motion.* Tell students that previewing the text, identifying important terms, and asking questions about these terms will help them better understand what a text is about. Model this technique by saying, **Here is a question I would ask myself before I read. "What words are used over and over in the text?"** (Things move.) **What clues do these words give me about the bold word *motion*?** (Sample answer: They tell me that motion and moving are related.)

Hard Push, Soft Push

NEXT GENERATION SCIENCE STANDARDS | DISCIPLINARY CORE IDEAS

PS2.A: Forces and Motion Pushes and pulls can have different strengths and directions. (K-PS2-1), (K-PS2-2)

PS3.C: Relationship Between Energy and Forces A bigger push or pull makes things speed up or slow down more quickly. (*secondary to K-PS2-1*)

Objectives Students will be able to:

- Identify that pushes can have different strengths and directions.
- Explain that a bigger push makes things speed up or slow down more quickly.

Science Vocabulary

push

ENGAGE

Tap Prior Knowledge

- Ask students to imagine that they are in the grocery store. Ask: **How do people make grocery carts move?** (by pushing them) Have students pretend to push a grocery cart, acting out the motions required to make it move. Ask: **What are some other things that you can push?** Have students share their ideas with the class.

EXPLORE

Preview the Lesson

- Display pages 6–7. Read the main heading aloud. Then direct students to observe the pictures on these pages. Ask: **What is happening in the large field?** (Possible answer: Two men are playing soccer. One man is kicking the ball to the other man.) Say: **Look at the girl.** Ask: **What is she doing?** (Possible answer: She is running; she is getting ready to kick the ball.) Invite students to share their experiences with kicking a ball or playing soccer. Ask: **Now that you have looked at the pictures and we have read the heading, what do you think the main topic of the lesson will be?** (Possible answer: The lesson title is about pushes. The pictures show people kicking balls. The lesson must be about how different kinds of kicks are different kinds of pushes.)

Set a Purpose and Read

- Have students listen to find out about hard and soft pushes.
- Have students follow along as you read aloud pages 6–7.

EXPLAIN

Define Push

- Make a pushing motion as you say the word *push*. Have students repeat the action and word. Reread the text, pointing to the word *push* each time it is read. Say: **A push moves something away. The man in the blue uniform gives the ball a push with his foot. The ball moves away from him.**
- Have students push an object, such as a book. Ask: **When you push the object, does it move away from you or toward you?** (It moves away from you.)

Describe Hard and Soft Pushes

- Point to the picture of the men in the field. Ask: **What has the man in the blue uniform pushed?** (a soccer ball) **What did he use to push the ball?** (He pushed the ball with his foot.) **What happened to the ball when he pushed it?** (It moved away from him; it rolled toward the other man.) Read aloud the caption text and discuss that the man pushed the ball softly, or gently. Ask: **How does the ball move when it is pushed softly?** (It moves slowly; it does not go far.)
- Point to the picture of the girl with the soccer ball. Ask: **What is the girl about to do?** (She is about to kick the ball; the girl is going to push the ball with her foot.) **What is going to happen to the ball?** (It is going to move away from the girl.) **What type of push is she going to give the ball—hard or soft?** (hard) **How do you know?** (Her foot is pulled far back from the ball. She looks like she will kick the ball hard when her foot hits the ball.) Read aloud

the caption text and discuss that a hard kick pushes the ball away faster and makes the ball travel a long way.

- Ask: **How is the push that the woman is using different from the push the man is using?** (The woman's push is harder; it makes the ball move faster and longer. The man's push is softer; it makes the ball move away slowly, and it does not go as far.) Say: **Think about giving a ball a hard push, and then giving the same ball a soft push. Both times, the ball rolls away from you. Which time will the ball slow down more quickly?** (Guide students to understand that the softer push will result in the ball slowing down sooner and more quickly than the harder push.)

ELABORATE

Find Out More About Pushes

Have students work in small groups to explore pushing objects with varying forces. Provide each group with two identical hardcover books. Have groups push one book gently across the floor and the other book harder. Ask groups to compare how far and fast the books moved. Encourage groups to try the same exploration with different objects. Students should record their observations in their science notebook.

Extend Your Thinking About Pushes in Nature

Have students work in small groups to find pictures of pushes in nature causing something to move, such as wind blowing leaves on a tree. Provide students with magazines and Internet resources to use for their research. Invite students to cut/print pictures to make a group poster of pushes in nature.

EVALUATE

Have students record their answer to the Wrap It Up question in their science notebook.

Wrap It Up!

1. **RESTATE How can you make a ball move fast and far?** (I can give the ball a hard kick, or push, to move the ball fast and far.)

SCIENCE MISCONCEPTIONS

Putting Things in Motion

A common misconception is that a force, such as a push, is needed in order for an object to remain in motion. Actually, if an object is in motion, it will continue moving in the same direction at the same speed unless a force changes its motion. Or, if an object is at rest, a force is needed to start it moving.

Suppose you push a ball along the ground. If no force acted on it, the ball would continue moving forever. However, the ball soon stops because the force of friction between the ball and the ground pushes back against the ball, slowing it.

READING CONNECTION

Identify the Main Topic

With prompting and support, identify the main topic and retell key details of a text.

Guide students to identify the main topic and retell key details of a text. For example, in the EXPLORE section as you preview the lesson with students, have students read the lesson title and tell what they observe in the pictures to help them find clues to the main topic of the lesson. In the EXPLAIN section when asking students to define *push*, guide students to use their own words to retell details from the text and captions to describe a push as a force that moves something away. Also in the EXPLAIN section when asking students to compare hard and soft pushes, guide students to use their own words to retell details from the text and captions to describe how soft pushes move objects more slowly and over a shorter distance and hard pushes move objects faster and farther.

Investigate

Hard and Soft Pushes

NEXT GENERATION SCIENCE STANDARDS | DISCIPLINARY CORE IDEAS

PS2.A: Forces and Motion Pushes and pulls can have different strengths and directions. (K-PS2-1), (K-PS2-2)

PS3.C: Relationship Between Energy and Forces A bigger push or pull makes things speed up or slow down more quickly. *(secondary to K-PS2-1)*

Objectives **Students will be able to:**

- Observe and record how the strength of a push can change motion.
- Observe that a bigger push makes things speed up or slow down more quickly.

CLASSROOM MANAGEMENT

Material ***For groups of 4:*** board (25 x 50 cm); 3 books; 1 small ball

Time 20 minutes

Advance Preparation Select 3 books to produce approximately the same slope for each group's ramp. Collect balls of approximately the same size made of the same material (rubber/plastic/wood) for each group.

Teaching Tips Before beginning the *Investigate*, remind students that they will not be throwing the ball, but only pushing it up the ramp. Model lab safety by wearing your safety goggles.

What to Expect Students will observe that the ball will roll only a short distance up the ramp when they use a small, or weak, push. It will roll most or all of the way up the ramp or off the ramp when they use a big, or strong, push. The ball will move in the direction of the push. A little push will make the ball move slowly. A strong push will make the ball move quickly.

ENGAGE

Tap Prior Knowledge

- Ask students to think about a time when they have pushed an object up a slope, or hill. Perhaps they have pushed a toy wheelbarrow or toy truck up a hill. Encourage them to share how their push affected the motion of the object. Review with students how the soccer players in the previous lesson pushed balls with their feet and what happened to the balls depending on the strength of the push they used.

EXPLORE

- Have students wear safety goggles.
- Guide students through the investigation. Read aloud pages 8–9 together.

My science notebook Help students make a table for recording their observations in their science notebook.

Example:

Hard and Soft Pushes

Type of Push	What I Predict	What Happened
hard		
soft		

- Show students the materials they will be using, having students match each pictured item to the real item as they say the name.
- Read aloud the heading, and then the *Investigate* question: *How does the strength of a push change motion?* Read aloud the steps on page 9. Tell students that they will follow these steps to answer the question. Move from group to group and clarify steps as necessary.
- Have students make predictions of what might happen to the ball during the investigation.

- During step 1, remind students that they want to make their ramp stable and will use this ramp for each trial of the investigation. Caution students not to push the ball so strongly that it moves past the top of the ramp. Stress that the goal is to use a force just strong enough to keep the ball on the ramp.
- For steps 2 and 3, respectively, ask: **What do you observe when you use a soft push? What do you observe when you use a hard push?** Remind students to record their observations for each type of push in their tables. Encourage students use pictures and words to describe what they observed.
- For step 4, have students discuss their findings with other members of their group. Encourage comparisons, asking probing questions such as: **Which type of push made the ball move faster? Slower? Which type of push made the ball move farther? Not as far?**

EXPLAIN

- Have each group review their predictions and compare them with what happened. Guide students to review the observations recorded in their tables and use them to explain their results. Ask: **What was different about the way the ball moved for hard pushes and soft pushes?** (A hard push made the ball move faster and farther up the ramp than a soft push.) **Why do you think the ball moved differently?** (Hard pushes move objects faster and farther than soft pushes.)
- As each group shares explanations and conclusions, encourage students to ask questions to increase understanding. Students should listen for other interpretations and ideas. Discuss possible reasons for any differences in results or explanations.

ELABORATE

- Have groups extend the investigation by exploring how the strength of a push affects how quickly a moving object will slow down and stop. Encourage groups to predict when a ball will slow more quickly—when given a hard push or when given a soft push. Have students record their predictions and results in their science notebook. Ask: **When did the ball slow more quickly—when given a hard push or when given a soft push?** (Given that the students are using the same ball both times and rolling it on the same surface, they should find that the ball given the smaller/softer push slows down more quickly than the ball given the bigger/harder push.)

EVALUATE

Have students record their answer to the Wrap It Up question in their science notebook.

Wrap It Up!

1. DRAW CONCLUSIONS **What made the ball move in different ways?** (The ball moved differently when I used different types of pushes. A hard push made the ball move faster and farther than a soft push.)

READING CONNECTION

Understand Unknown Words

With prompting and support, ask and answer questions about unknown words in a text.

Guide students to ask and answer questions about unknown words. As you begin the EXPLORE section, direct students to step 1. Point out the word *ramp* and the accompanying picture. Ask if they have any questions about what a ramp is. Explain that when books and boards are arranged as shown in the picture, they make a ramp. Ask students to share examples of ramps they have seen. (Students may cite ramps used to load trucks or moving vans, ramps for wheelchairs, and so on.)

Weak Pull, Strong Pull

NEXT GENERATION SCIENCE STANDARDS | DISCIPLINARY CORE IDEAS
PS2.A: Forces and Motion Pushes and pulls can have different strengths and directions. (K-PS2-1), (K-PS2-2)

Objective Students will be able to:
- Identify that pulls can have different strengths and directions.

Science Vocabulary
pull

ENGAGE

Tap Prior Knowledge

- Have students name ways that they have moved things today. Suggest that students think about the things they did before coming to school (e.g., opening cabinets or drawers to get food and clothing, opening and closing doors to leave the house or to come into the school). For each example, ask: **Did you use a push or pull to move it?** Have students describe what they did and the direction the object moved.

EXPLORE

Preview the Lesson

- Display pages 10–11. Have students share what they observe in the large picture as well as the small inset picture. Ask: **What is happening in the large picture?** (Possible answer: A man on skis is moving a big sled; a rope from the sled is tied around the man's waist, and he is climbing up the snowy hill.)
- Ask: **What is happening in the small picture?** (Possible answer: A girl is walking up a snowy hill holding onto a rope that is attached to a sled; she is pulling the sled behind her.)

Set a Purpose and Read

- Read the main heading. Tell students to listen to find out about weak and strong pulls.
- Have students follow along as you read aloud pages 10–11.

EXPLAIN

Define Pull

- Make a pulling motion as you say the word *pull* aloud to the class. Have students repeat the action and word. Reread the text on pages 10–11, pointing to the word *pull* each time it is read. Say: **A pull moves something toward you. The girl pulls her sled up the hill. The sled moves toward her.**
- Have students pull an object, such as a chair. Ask: **When you pull the chair, does it move away from you or toward you?** (toward you) Have students make pushing and pulling motions. Explain that a push is the opposite of a pull.

Describe Weak and Strong Pulls

- Direct students to look again at the pictures. Point to the inset picture of the girl. Ask: **What is the girl doing?** (She is pulling a sled with a rope.) **What happens to the sled as she pulls it?** (The sled moves toward the girl up the hill.) Read aloud the caption and discuss that the girl is using a weak pull to move her sled. Ask: **Why can the sled move with a weak pull?** (The sled is not heavy; it is a light sled.)
- Point to the picture of the man pulling the sled. Ask: **What is the man doing?** (He is pulling a sled up a steep hill.) **How is he pulling the sled?** (The sled is attached to a rope, and the rope is tied around the man's waist. As the man moves up the hill, he is pulling the sled behind him.) **Does it look easy or difficult to pull the man's sled?** (difficult) **What clues make you think it is difficult for the man to pull the sled?** (The man is leaning forward; he is digging his skis/feet and poles into the snow.) **Why do you think it might be difficult to pull the sled?** (His sled is heavy.) Read aloud the caption and discuss how the man needs to use a strong pull in order to move his heavy sled toward him.
- Ask: **How is the girl's pull different from the man's pull?** (The girl uses a weak pull to move her sled. The man uses a strong pull to move his sled. The girl's pull is much easier to do than the man's pull.)

ELABORATE

Find Out More About Pulls

My science notebook Have students work in groups pulling different objects around the classroom. Have groups choose two different things to pull, one noticeably heavier than the other. Invite students to take turns pulling their objects and describing their pulls as weak or strong. Students should draw pictures of each object in their science notebook and label each as requiring either a weak or strong pull to be moved.

Extend Your Thinking About Pulls

My science notebook Ask: **What do you pull on to get dressed each morning?** Have students think about what they did to get dressed that morning. Discuss how most items of clothing require a pull in order to get them on. Review the various items as a class, making a list on the board. (Sample answers: shirts, pants, skirts, socks, shoes) Have students share whether certain items require a stronger pull than others to get on, such as getting a shirt over the head or getting a sock on a foot.

EVALUATE

My science notebook Have students record their answer to the Wrap It Up question in their science notebook.

Wrap It Up!

ANALYZE **How can you tell that the girl's sled is easy for her to pull?** (Possible answer: She is standing up straight and does not look like she is struggling to pull the sled.)

DIFFERENTIATED INSTRUCTION

Extra Support Place a collection of small classroom objects on the floor. Some objects should have wheels, some should be very light, and others a bit heavier. Have students experiment with pulling each object with weak and strong pulls.

Challenge Have students use a dump truck or another type of truck that can hold objects in the back to explore what types of pulls are required for heavier and lighter loads. Provide small blocks, having students places a few at a time in the back of the truck and then pulling the truck with weak pulls. Encourage students to continue adding blocks, noting when they need to increase their force from a weak to a strong pull in order to make the truck move.

READING CONNECTION

Describe the Relationship

With prompting and support, describe the relationship between illustrations and the text in which they appear (e.g., what person, place, thing, or idea in the text an illustration depicts).

Guide students to describe the relationship between illustrations and the text in which they appear. For example, in the EXPLAIN section as students examine the illustrations, have them look for clues as to how hard or easy it seems to be for the girl and man to pull their respective sleds. Reread the main heading to remind students that they are looking for clues as to which requires a strong pull, and which requires a weak pull. Then have students identify the clues to the types of pulls in each picture.

Investigate

Weak and Strong Pulls

NEXT GENERATION SCIENCE STANDARDS | DISCIPLINARY CORE IDEAS

PS2.A: Forces and Motion Pushes and pulls can have different strengths and directions. (K-PS2-1), (K-PS2-2)

PS3.C: Relationship Between Energy and Forces A bigger push or pull makes things speed up or slow down more quickly. (*secondary to K-PS2-1*)

Objectives **Students will be able to:**

- Observe and record how the strength of a pull can change motion.
- Observe that a stronger pull makes things speed up or slow down more quickly.

CLASSROOM MANAGEMENT

Materials ***For groups of 4:*** board (25 × 50 cm); 3 books; small toy car; string ***For teacher use:*** tape

Time 20 minutes

Advance Preparation Select three books to produce approximately the same slope for each ramp. For each group, cut a piece of string 1 meter long. Tape the string securely to the underside of the toy car so that the car will roll smoothly and the string will not get tangled in the wheels.

Teaching Tips Explain to students that as they are pulling the car, they should give a quick pull of the string for both the weak and strong forces, and then let the string go. Students should not keep pulling the car up the ramp. Demonstrate this technique for students before they begin the investigation steps. Model lab safety by wearing your Safety goggles.

What to Expect Students will observe that the car will move only a short distance up the ramp with a weak pull. It will roll farther up the ramp with a strong pull. The car will always move in the direction of the pull. A weak pull will make the car move slowly. A strong pull will make the car move quickly.

ENGAGE

Tap Prior Knowledge

- Ask students to think about a time when they have pulled an object up a slope, or hill. Perhaps they have pulled a wagon up a hill, or dragged a sled behind them like the girl on page 10. Encourage them to share how their pull affected the motion of the object. Review with students how the people in the previous lesson pulled sleds up slopes using ropes, and what types of pulls they used to make the sleds move.

EXPLORE

- Have students wear safety goggles.
- Guide students through the investigation. Read aloud pages 12–13 together.

My science notebook — Help students make a table for recording their observations in their science notebook.

Example:

Weak and Strong Pulls

Type of Pull	What I Predict	What Happened
weak		
strong		

- Show students the materials they will be using, having students match each pictured item to the actual object as they say the name.
- Read aloud the main heading, and then the investigation question: *How does the strength of a pull change motion?* Read aloud the steps of the investigation on page 13. Tell students that they will follow these steps to answer the question. Move from group to group and clarify steps if necessary.

- Have students make predictions of what might happen to the toy car during the investigation. During step 1, remind students that they want to make their ramp stable and will use this ramp for each trial of the investigation. Caution students not to pull the car so strongly that it moves past the top of the ramp. Stress that the goal is to use a force just strong enough to keep the car on the ramp.
- For steps 2 and 3, respectively, ask: **What do you observe when you use a weak pull? What do you observe when you use a strong pull?** Remind students to record their observations for each type of pull in their tables. Encourage students to use pictures and words to describe what they observe.
- For step 4, have students discuss their findings with other members of their group. Encourage comparisons, asking probing questions such as: **Which type of pull made the car move faster? Slower? Which type of pull made the car move farther? Not as far?**

EXPLAIN

- Have each group review their predictions and compare them with what happened. Guide students to review the observations recorded in their tables and use them to explain their results. Ask: **What was different about the way the car moved for weak pulls and strong pulls?** (A strong pull made the car move faster and farther up the ramp than a weak pull.) **Why do you think the car moved differently?** (Strong pulls move an object faster and farther than weak pulls.)
- As each group shares explanations and conclusions, encourage students to ask questions to increase understanding. Students should listen for other interpretations and ideas. Discuss possible reasons for any differences in results or explanations.

ELABORATE

- Have groups extend the investigation by exploring how the strength of a pull affects how quickly a moving object will slow down and stop. Encourage groups to predict when a ball will slow more quickly—when given a hard pull or when given a soft pull. Have students record their predictions and results in their science notebook. Ask: **When did the ball slow more quickly—when given a hard pull or when given a soft pull?** (Given that students are using the same ball both times and rolling it on the same surface, they should find that the ball given the smaller/softer pull slows down more quickly than the ball given the bigger/harder pull.)

EVALUATE

Have students record their answer to the Wrap It Up question in their science notebook.

Wrap It Up!

1. DESCRIBE **What made the car move in different ways?** (Possible answer: Using weak or strong pulls made the car move in different ways. When I gave the string a weak pull, the car moved slowly and not very far. When I gave the string a strong pull, the car move faster and farther.)

READING CONNECTION

Describe the Relationship

With prompting and support, describe the relationship between illustrations and the text in which they appear (e.g., what person, place, thing, or idea in the text an illustration depicts).

Guide students to describe the relationship between illustrations and the text. For example, in the EXPLORE section as you introduce the *Investigate* activity, direct students to the materials list. Point to the picture of each material as you read its name. Ask: **What is the purpose of this section?** (It tells me what materials I need to use to complete the activity.) **How do the pictures help you?** (The pictures show me what each object I will be using looks like.)

Starting and Stopping

NEXT GENERATION SCIENCE STANDARDS | DISCIPLINARY CORE IDEAS

PS2.A: Forces and Motion Pushing or pulling on an object can change the speed or direction of its motion and can start or stop it. (K-PS2-1). (K-PS2-2)

PS2.B: Types of Interactions When objects touch or collide, they push on one another and can change motion. (K-PS2-1)

Objectives Students will be able to:

- Explain that pushing or pulling on an object can start or stop it from moving.
- Explain that when objects touch or collide, they push on one another and can change motion.

ENGAGE

Tap Prior Knowledge

- Have students think about a time when they played ball with a friend. Ask: **How did you get the ball to your friend?** (Student answers will vary. Possible answer: I kicked the ball to my friend; I threw the ball to my friend.) **Did you use a push or a pull to move the ball?** (Possible answer: I pushed the ball with my foot; I pushed the ball with my hand.) Discuss other sports that students have played that use a push or a pull to move something from one player to another.

EXPLORE

Preview the Lesson

- Display pages 14–15. Have students share what they observe happening in both pictures. Direct students to pay attention to the motions that the football players are performing. Point to the picture of the player in the red jersey and ask: **What is happening in this picture?** Have students share their answers. Discuss the position of the player's hands and the action he is preparing to take using the ball.

Set a Purpose and Read

- Read the main heading. Have students listen to find out about starting and stopping objects in motion.
- Have students follow along as you read aloud pages 14–15.

EXPLAIN

Discuss Pushes and Pulls That Start and Stop Motion

- Reread pages 14–15. Say: **These players are using pushes and pulls to play football.** Direct students to look at the football player in the red jersey. Read the caption aloud and ask: **What is this player doing with the football?** (He is holding it in his hand; he is getting ready to throw the ball.) **Is the ball moving yet?** (Not yet.) **What will make the ball start to move?** (The player will push the ball with his hand to start it moving; the player will throw the ball.) **In what direction will the ball move when he pushes it?** (It will move forward; it will move away from him.)
- Point to the picture of the football player in the blue jersey. Read the caption aloud and ask: **What is this player doing with his hands?** (He is holding the football he caught.) **What happened to the ball?** (The ball landed in the player's hands.) **Did the player start or stop the ball from moving?** (He is stopped it from moving.) Explain that when the ball lands in the player's hand, the player is pushing on the ball with his hands to stop it from moving.

Explain How Collisions Can Change Motion

- Review with students the different ways that the players are starting and stopping the footballs on pages 14–15. Ask: **What parts of their bodies are the players using to start and stop the football?** (They are using their hands.) **How are their hands starting and stopping the motion?** (Possible answer: One player is pushing the ball with his hands to throw it away from him. The other player caught the ball with his hands, pushing against the ball and stopping it from moving.)
- Discuss with students that when two objects bang into each other, it is called a collision. When two objects collide, they push on each other, changing motion. Demonstrate this action by using a small ball or object and tossing it

from one hand to the other. Say: **Watch as I throw the ball with my right hand. When the ball hits my left hand, it stops moving. The ball collided with my left hand and stopped moving.** Point to the picture of the player in the blue jersey. Say: **This player stopped the football using his hands. The ball collided with his hands and stopped moving. The ball pushed on his hands while his hands pushed back on the ball.** Invite students to try moving an object with one hand to the other, demonstrating how their hands and the object collide, pushing on each other and stopping motion.

ELABORATE

Extend Your Thinking About Football and Motion

Have students discuss what they know about the game of football. Share that the players do a lot of running and colliding while also throwing and catching a football. Have students draw pictures of something that happens during a football game. If necessary, provide Internet resources for students to watch or view images of football games in action. Encourage students to find images of starting the ball, stopping the ball, and any collisions that might change motion.

EVALUATE

Have students record their answers to the Wrap It Up questions in their science notebook.

Wrap It Up!

1. EXPLAIN **How can you make a ball start moving?** (I can throw a ball with a push of my hand; I can kick a ball with a push of my foot.)
2. EXPLAIN **How can you make a ball stop moving?** (I can stop a ball by catching it and pushing against it with my hand; I can stop a ball rolling by pushing against it with my foot.)

ELL SUPPORT

Starting and Stopping Motion

Beginning Have students sort pictures of people pushing or pulling on objects to start or stop motion. Ask either/or questions about the type of movement, such as: *Is the girl starting or stopping the ball? Is she using a push or a pull?*

Intermediate Help students identify in their pictures whether the person is starting or stopping the motion and the type of force being used. Provide sentence frames, such as: *He/She (stops) the (ball) with a (push). He/She (starts) the (wagon) with a (pull).*

Advanced Encourage students to use descriptive words when writing sentences about the pictures they found. For example, they might write, *The girl stops the ball with a push.* Have them look at the picture and think of a way to describe the movement in greater detail.

READING CONNECTION

Describe Connections

With prompting and support, describe the connection between two individuals, events, ideas, or pieces of information in a text.

Guide students to describe the connection between ideas or pieces of information in a text. For example, in the EXPLAIN section when asking students to describe what the football players are doing, guide students to describe the connection between a push that starts the ball in motion and the push that stops the ball from moving. Ask: **What do starting and stopping the ball have in common?** (Guide students to understand that they both involve pushes.)

Investigate

Starting and Stopping

NEXT GENERATION SCIENCE STANDARDS | DISCIPLINARY CORE IDEAS

PS2.A: Forces and Motion Pushing or pulling on an object can change the speed or direction of its motion and can start or stop it. (K-PS2-1), (K-PS2-2)

PS2.B: Types of Interactions When objects touch or collide, they push on one another and can change motion. (K-PS2-1)

Objectives Students will be able to:

- Observe and record how pushing and pulling on an object can change the direction of its motion and can start or stop it.
- Identify that when objects touch or collide, they push on one another and can change motion.

CLASSROOM MANAGEMENT

Materials ***For groups of 2:*** small rubber ball

Time 20 minutes

Teaching Tips Remind students that when rolling the ball toward a partner, they should keep the ball on the ground and use enough force so that the ball reaches their partner's hands, which will then stop the ball.

What to Expect Students will observe that the ball starts moving when one student rolls it by giving it a push with his/her hands. The ball stays in motion until it reaches the partner's hands, which stops the ball when the ball and hands touch, or collide. When partners switch roles, they will observe the same starting and stopping actions, but this time, the ball will be traveling in the opposite direction than it did in the first trial. Students should conclude that pushing a ball can start or stop it, and that when their hands and the ball collide, the ball stops and can be redirected by another push of the hands.

ENGAGE

Tap Prior Knowledge

- Ask students to think back to the previous lesson and the two football players. Remind students of the one player throwing the ball and the other player catching the ball. Ask: **How did the player start the football moving?** (by throwing it; by pushing it away with his hands) **How did the other player stop the football from moving?** (By catching it; when the ball and his hands collided, they pushed against each other and the ball stopped.)

EXPLORE

- Guide students through the investigation. Read aloud pages 16–17 together.

My science notebook: Help students make a table for recording their observations in their science notebook.

Example:

Starting and Stopping

Roll the Ball	What I Predict	What Happened
Trial #1		
Trial #2		

- Read aloud the main heading and then the investigation question: *How can you make a ball start and stop moving?* Read aloud the steps of the investigation on page 17. Remind students that they will follow these steps to answer the question. Move from group to group and clarify steps as necessary.
- Have students make predictions of what might happen to the ball during the investigation.
- For steps 2 and 3, remind students to roll the ball with enough force to reach their partner so that their partner has to stop the rolling using his/her hands. Caution students not to roll the

ball so strongly that it rolls or bounces away from their partner. Ask: **What did you do to start the ball rolling? What did your partner do to stop the ball from moving?**

- For step 4, students should switch roles and repeat steps 2 and 3. Remind students to record their observations for each trial in their tables. Encourage students to use pictures and words to describe what they observed.
- Have partners discuss their findings. Ask probing questions, such as: **How did you start the ball? What happened when your partner's hands collided with the ball? How did you change the direction of the ball? Did you use pushes or pulls to change the motion of the ball each time?**

EXPLAIN

- Have pairs review their predictions and compare them with what happened. Guide students to review the observations they recorded in their tables and use them to explain their results. Ask: **What did you do to start and stop the ball from moving?** (We started the ball with a push to roll it. We stopped the ball with our hands. The ball and our hands pushed against each other as they touched. This stopped the ball.) **What was different when you switched roles?** (We started and stopped the ball the same way each time. But, my partner started the ball and I stopped it, and the ball rolled in the opposite direction than it did the first time because this time, my partner was rolling the ball toward me.)
- As pairs share explanations and conclusions, encourage students to ask questions to increase understanding. Students should listen for other interpretations and ideas. Discuss possible reasons for any differences in results or explanations.

ELABORATE

- Have pairs continue the investigation to further support their conclusions. Provide additional materials for students to push toward each other such as toy trains, cars, or other small objects that can roll. Encourage groups to predict what will happen to each object when rolled back and forth between partners. Suggest that students vary the speed at which they roll the ball and analyze differences when the ball is rolled quickly or slowly.
- Have students record their predictions and results in their science notebook. Revisit students' conclusions from the original investigation. Ask: **Did you start and stop these object the same way as you did when you rolled the ball? How did changing the speed at which you rolled the ball change how the ball moved?**

EVALUATE

My science notebook

Have students record their answer to the Wrap It Up question in their science notebook.

Wrap It Up!

1. CONCLUDE **How can you start and stop motion?** (I can use a push of my hands to start something moving. I can also use a push of my hands to stop something from moving.)

READING CONNECTION

Describe Connections

With prompting and support, describe the connection between two individuals, events, ideas, or pieces of information in a text.

In the EXPLAIN section after reading aloud the steps, guide students to describe the connection between the steps in this *Investigate* activity. Ask students to tell what the action is in each step and what the partners will be doing with the ball.

Changing Direction

NEXT GENERATION SCIENCE STANDARDS | DISCIPLINARY CORE IDEAS

PS2.A: Forces and Motion Pushing or pulling on an object can change the speed or direction of its motion and can start or stop it. (K-PS2-1), (K-PS2-2)

PS2.B: Types of Interactions When objects touch or collide, they push on one another and can change motion. (K-PS2-1)

Objectives **Students will be able to:**

- Identify that pushing or pulling on an object can change the direction of its motion.
- Explain that when objects touch or collide, they push on one another and can change motion.

Science Vocabulary

direction

ENGAGE

Tap Prior Knowledge

- Ask students to think about different sports that they have played which involve either hitting or kicking a ball. Discuss a baseball player hitting a ball with a bat or a soccer player kicking a ball with his or her foot. Say: **A pitcher throws a ball toward the batter.** Ask: **What does the batter try to do?** (hit the ball) Discuss with students what can happen to the ball when it is hit. Invite students who have played or watched baseball games to share what they know about the different ways that a baseball moves during the game.

EXPLORE

Preview the Lesson

- Display pages 18–19. Have students share what they observe happening in both pictures. Point to the picture of the tennis player and ask: **What do you notice about the tennis player?** Have students share their answers. Discuss the ball's motion as well as the position of the tennis racket as the player is preparing to hit the ball.

Set a Purpose and Read

- Read the heading. Tell students to listen to find out about changing the direction of objects in motion.
- Have students follow along as you read aloud pages 18–19.

EXPLAIN

Define Direction

- Direct students to revisit the pictures on pages 18–19. Reread the heading and text aloud, pointing to the word *direction* each time it is read. Point to the tennis ball and say: **The tennis player hit the ball with a racket. The ball follows a path as it moves. The path that the ball follows is its direction.**
- Invite a volunteer to walk in a straight line from one location in the classroom to another, such as from the board to the door. Say: **(Student's name) is walking from the board to the door. (Student's name) is following a path to the door. (Student's name) is walking in the direction of the door.** Have other students walk in different directions and discuss how each student is following a certain path, and that that path is the direction in which the student is moving.

Describe How Forces Can Change the Direction of Moving Objects

- Point to the picture of the girl playing tennis. Read the caption aloud. Say: **The tennis ball is moving toward the girl.** Ask: **What is the girl getting ready to do with her racket?** (She is getting ready to hit the ball.) Explain to students that in the game of tennis, people use rackets to hit the tennis ball back and forth over a net in the center of the court.
- Ask: **What will happen to the ball when the racket hits it?** (The ball will move away from the tennis player.) **Will the ball be moving in the same direction anymore? Why or why not?** (No. The ball was moving toward the girl. When she hits the ball with her racket, the ball will move away from her. The ball changes direction.)
- Direct students to look at the inset picture of the hockey player. Read the caption text and say: **Hockey players use a stick to hit a puck along the ice toward a goal. This player is trying to get the puck to change direction.** Ask: **How can the hockey player change the**

direction of the puck? (He can hit the puck with his stick.) **What happens to the puck when it hits the wall?** (It bangs into the wall and then moves away from the wall. It changes direction.) Discuss how a hockey puck slides along the ice and when it hits, or collides, with something, the puck's direction changes.

ELABORATE

Find Out More About Changing Motion

My science notebook

Have students use small classroom objects that slide or roll well on the floor to explore how objects change direction when colliding with something else. Have pairs of students sit close to a wall and slide or roll the object with medium force toward the wall. Ask: **What happened to your object when it hit the wall?** Students should note that their objects hit and then bounce back or move away from the wall in a different direction. Have students use drawings and words to document their observations in their science notebook.

Extend Your Thinking About Motion and Direction

My science notebook

Discuss with students how baseball players use a bat to hit a ball thrown at them by a pitcher. Ask: **Do you think a batter can control the direction the ball moves after he or she hits it?** Students may have varying answers, but all should understand that the batter changes the direction in which the ball is moving when he hits it. Provide small groups with sports magazines and Internet resources for finding pictures of baseball players hitting balls into the outfield. Encourage students to find more than one picture and compare the direction the ball is heading in each visual. Discuss how the ball can move in all different directions once hit, and that batters practice so that they can direct the ball in different ways.

EVALUATE

My science notebook

Have students record their answer to the Wrap It Up question in their science notebook.

Wrap It Up!

1. EXPLAIN **How do tennis players change the direction of the ball?** (They hit the ball with their rackets. The ball moves toward a player. When the player hits the ball, it moves away from that player in a different direction.)

TEACHING WITH TECHNOLOGY

Changing a Ball's Direction

Project the lesson on a whiteboard. Have volunteers come up to the board to circle objects traveling in one direction. (tennis ball, hockey puck) Have a second set of volunteers come to the board and draw an "X" over the tools that the players will use to change the direction of the ball and puck, respectively. (tennis racket, hockey stick) Invite a third set of volunteers to come to the board and draw an arrow showing the direction the ball and puck might travel once hit. Discuss how these moving objects keep moving in one direction unless something hits them, changing their traveling directions.

READING CONNECTION

Describe Connections

With prompting and support, describe the connection between two individuals, events, ideas, or pieces of information in a text.

Guide students to describe the connection between two pieces of information in a text. For example, in the EXPLAIN section when having students explain how forces can change an object's direction, have students describe the connection between the girl hitting the tennis ball with her racket and the ball's direction changing. Also in the EXPLAIN section when having students explain what happens to the puck when it hits the wall, have students describe how the puck's direction changes when it is hit with the stick or collides with the wall.

Investigate

Changing Direction

NEXT GENERATION SCIENCE STANDARDS | DISCIPLINARY CORE IDEAS

PS2.A: Forces and Motion Pushing or pulling on an object can change the speed or direction of its motion and can start or stop it. (K-PS2-1), (K-PS2-2)

PS2.B: Types of Interactions When objects touch or collide, they push on one another and can change motion. (K-PS2-1)

Objectives **Students will be able to:**

- Observe and record how pushing and pulling on an object can change the direction of its motion.
- Identify that when objects touch or collide, they push on one another and can change motion.

CLASSROOM MANAGEMENT

Materials ***For groups of 2:*** small rubber ball

Time 20 minutes

Teaching Tips Make sure that students sit close enough to the wall so that when they roll their ball, it reaches the wall with enough force to collide and roll away in a different direction. Model lab safety by wearing your safety goggles.

What to Expect Students will observe that when they roll a ball toward a wall, the ball will collide with the wall and then roll away from the wall. The ball's direction will change each time students roll it into the wall, but the new direction the ball takes will depend upon the angle at which the ball was originally rolled. Students will discover that rolling the ball straight into the wall will send the ball back to the student. Rolling the ball toward the wall at an angle will send the ball rolling away from the wall in a different direction, but not back to the student.

ENGAGE

Tap Prior Knowledge

- Have student think back to the previous lesson with the tennis player and hockey player. Remind students of the tennis ball moving toward the girl with the racket. Ask: **How can the girl change the direction of the ball?** (She can hit the ball with her tennis racket.) **In which direction will the ball move then?** (The ball will move away from the girl and toward the other side of the court.)

EXPLORE

- Have students wear safety goggles.
- Guide students through the investigation. Read aloud pages 20–21.

My science notebook: Help students make a table for recording their observations in their science notebook.

Example:

Changing Direction

Roll the Ball	What I Predict	What Happened
Trial #1		
Trial #2		
Trial #3		
Trial #4		

- Read aloud the heading, and then the investigation question: *How can you change the direction of a moving object?* Read aloud the steps on page 21. Tell students that they will follow these steps to answer the question. Move from group to group and clarify steps as necessary.
- Have students make predictions of what might happen to the ball during the investigation. For all steps, remind students that they want to make sure they roll the ball with enough force to reach the wall, collide with the wall, and roll away from the wall. Caution students not to roll the ball so strongly that it rolls or bounces away from their intended target.
- For steps 1, 2, and 3, ask: **What happened when the ball hit the wall? In which direction did the ball roll after hitting the wall?** Remind students to record their observations for each trial in their tables. Encourage students to use pictures and words to describe what they observed.

- For step 4, remind students to plan a way that is different from the first three trials that they completed. Students should try their idea and record results in their tables.
- Have partners discuss their findings. Ask probing questions such as:
  - **What happened to the ball each time it collided with the wall?**
  - **How did you make the ball roll straight back?**
  - **In what other directions did the ball travel after it hit the wall?**
  - **What did you notice about the direction you rolled the ball and the direction it traveled in after hitting the wall?**

EXPLAIN

- Have pairs review their predictions and compare them with what happened. Guide students to review the observations they recorded in their tables and use them to explain their results. Ask: **What did you need to do to get the ball to roll back to you?** (We sat with the wall straight ahead of us. Then we rolled the ball in a straight line directly toward the wall.) **What was different when you changed the way you rolled the ball?** (When we rolled the ball from different places, such as from one side or another verses straight ahead, the ball hit the wall and rolled away in different directions. It did not roll back to us.) **How can you change the direction of a moving ball?** (I can make it hit something else, which will make the ball change direction. I can also make the ball bounce off the wall in different directions by changing my position and the way I roll the ball.)
- As pairs share explanations and conclusions, encourage students to ask questions to increase understanding. Students should listen for other interpretations and ideas. Discuss possible reasons for any differences in results or explanations.

ELABORATE

- Have pairs continue the investigation to further support their conclusions. Provide students with a hardcover book to use as their "wall." Then have partners predict what will happen when they roll the ball toward the book. Direct students to change the position of the book each time instead of changing the direction of the roll. Pairs should try this several times.
- Have students record their results in their science notebook. Revisit students' conclusions from the original investigation. Ask: **Were you able to get the ball to roll back to you as you did in the original investigation? In what other directions did the ball travel when you changed the position of the book?** Encourage students to discuss how their results support their conclusions from the original investigation.

EVALUATE

My science notebook

Have students record their answer to the Wrap It Up question in their science notebook.

Wrap It Up!

1. **EXPLAIN How did you change the direction of the ball?** (Sample answer: I rolled the ball toward the wall. When it hit the wall, it changed direction and rolled away from the wall. I was able to make the ball roll in different directions by changing the place where I sat when I rolled the ball and by rolling the ball from different directions.)

READING CONNECTION

Describe the Relationship

With prompting and support, describe the relationship between illustrations and the text in which they appear (e.g., what person, place, thing, or idea in the text an illustration depicts).

Guide students to describe the relationship between illustrations and text. For example, in the EXPLORE section when reading through the steps shown on page 21, point out the picture in step 1. Say: **Look at the picture with step 1. What does it show you?** (The picture shows two students rolling a ball toward a wall.) **What does the step tell you to do?** (Work with a partner. Roll the ball toward a wall.) **How are the text and the picture connected?** (The picture shows what the text described in words.) Repeat this sequence using the picture and text in step 3.

Changing Speed

NEXT GENERATION SCIENCE STANDARDS | DISCIPLINARY CORE IDEAS

PS2.A: Forces and Motion Pushing or pulling on an object can change the speed or direction of its motion and can start or stop it. (K-PS2-1), (K-PS2-2)

PS2.B: Types of Interactions When objects collide, they push on one another and can change motion. (K-PS2-1)

Objectives Students will be able to:

- Identify that pushing or pulling on an object can change the speed of its motion.
- Explain that when objects touch or collide, they push on one another and can change motion.

Science Vocabulary

speed

ENGAGE

Tap Prior Knowledge

- Ask students to think about when they were rolling the ball to change its direction during the *Investigate* activity. Ask: **Did you roll the ball with a strong or weak push? How did the ball roll after it hit the wall?** Have students share their experiences. Discuss what other ways players could control the motion of a ball when playing sports such as soccer, volleyball, basketball, tennis, football, and baseball.

EXPLORE

Preview the Lesson

- Show pages 22–23. Have students share what they observe happening in both pictures. Point to each picture of the batters and ask: **What is happening here?** Have students share their answers. Discuss how in baseball, there is a person with a bat trying to the hit the ball away from them, as is shown in these pictures.

Set a Purpose and Read

- Read the heading. Tell students to listen to find out about changing the speed of objects in motion.
- Have students follow along as you read aloud pages 22–23.

EXPLAIN

Define Speed

- Have students revisit the pictures on pages 22–23. Reread the heading and text aloud, pointing to the word *speed* each time it is read. Point to the large picture of the batter hitting the ball. Say: **The batter hits the ball hard. The ball moves fast. Speed is how fast something is moving.**
- Have students experiment with moving at different speeds. First invite a small group of students to walk slowly toward the door and then back to their seats. Say: **You all walked slowly. You were moving at a slow speed.** Invite a second small group of students to walk quickly toward the door and then back to their seats. Say: **You all walked quickly. You were moving at a faster speed.** Have students share other thoughts about objects they know of that travel at varying speeds, such as cars, trucks, planes, and so on.

Describe Changing Speed

- Direct students' attention to the picture of the batter on page 22 and reread the caption. Explain that in baseball, a pitcher throws the ball at a fast speed and batters try to hit the ball with different strengths and in different directions. Say: **The pitcher threw the baseball toward this batter. The batter swings his bat and the bat and ball collide. The bat gives the ball a hard hit, or push.** Ask: **What happens to the ball after the bat and ball collide?** (The ball moves away from the bat.) **In this picture does the ball move slowly or quickly away from the bat?** (quickly) **Why do you think it moves quickly?** (Because the batter hit the ball hard; a hard push moves a ball faster than a soft push.)
- Direct students' attention to the inset picture of the batter. Read the caption text aloud. Say: **This batter uses his bat to give the ball a soft hit, or push.** Ask: **What does the soft hit do to the ball?** (It makes the ball move slowly away from the bat.) **Why does it move slowly?** (Because

the batter hit the ball softly; a soft push moves a ball slower than a hard push.)

- Discuss with students the way the ball's speed can change after the bat and ball collide. Ask: **Do you think the baseball is thrown at the batters quickly or slowly? Explain.** (I think that the balls are moving quickly toward the batters. You would have to throw the ball hard to get it from the pitcher to the batter.) **Which type of hit can make the ball's speed become faster?** (a hard hit) **Which type of hit can make the ball's speed become slower?** (a soft hit) **How can the type of hit change a ball's speed?** (Harder hits, or pushes, can make a ball's speed get faster; softer hits can make a ball's speed get slower.)

ELABORATE

Find Out More About Pitches

My science notebook Have students work in small groups to explore the varying speeds used to pitch baseballs. Help students use Internet resources about Major League Baseball to discover how pitchers control the speed of the ball when they throw. Help students read different speeds and explain that "miles per hour" (mph) is used to describe a baseball's speed once in motion. Have students list different speeds of pitches from fastest to slowest and discuss how a pitcher uses harder pushes for a faster pitch and softer pushes for a slower pitch.

Extend Your Thinking About Changing Speeds

My science notebook Have students think about a time when they have ridden a bicycle or scooter. Ask: **How did you make your bicycle or scooter go faster or slower?** Invite students to share their experiences. Direct students to describe the methods they used to change the speed of their bicycle or scooter, using either a change in pedaling or pushing strength depending on what they were riding. Have students draw a picture and write words describing the different ways they ride and change speeds as they go.

EVALUATE

My science notebook Have students record their answer to the Wrap It Up question in their science notebook.

Wrap It Up!

1. **DEFINE** **What is speed?** (Speed is how fast something is moving.)

DIFFERENTIATED INSTRUCTION

Extra Support Have students discuss the different ways a baseball player can change the speed of a moving ball. Remind students that a pitcher throws a ball at a quick speed toward a batter. Ask: **What should the batter do to make the ball move more slowly?** (The batter should give the ball a soft hit, or push, with the bat.) **What should the batter do to make the ball move more quickly?** (The batter should give the ball a very hard hit, or push, with the bat.)

Challenge Have students make a list of different sports that involve a ball or puck that is pushed or pulled to change its speed throughout the game. Encourage students to discuss what equipment is used to change the speed of the ball or puck and what players need to do to change the speed of these moving objects.

READING CONNECTION

Describe the Relationship

With prompting and support, describe the relationship between illustrations and the text in which they appear. (e.g., what person, place, thing, or idea in the text an illustration depicts).

Guide students to describe the relationship between illustrations and the text. For example, in the EXPLAIN section after students have used the caption copy to explain how the strength of the push, or hit, changes the speed of the ball, say: **Which picture shows a soft hit? Which shows a hard hit? How do you know?** (Students should indicate that the pictures show the different hits, and the captions explain how each hit makes the ball move.)

Investigate

Changing Speed

NEXT GENERATION SCIENCE STANDARDS | DISCIPLINARY CORE IDEAS

PS2.A: Forces and Motion Pushing or pulling on an object can change the speed or direction of its motion and can start or stop it. (K-PS2-1), (K-PS2-2)

Objective **Students will be able to:**

- Observe and record how pushing or pulling on an object can change the speed of its motion.

CLASSROOM MANAGEMENT

Materials ***For groups of 4:*** board (25 x 50 cm); 3 books; small toy car

Time 15 minutes

Advance Preparation Select three books to produce approximately the same slope for each ramp.

Teaching Tips Explain to students that when putting the car at the top of each ramp, they will simply let the car go. They should not push the car or apply any force to make the car roll. Model lab safety by wearing your safety goggles.

What to Expect Students will observe that when they release the car down the ramp made with 1 book, the car will travel at a slower speed than when they release the car down the ramp made with 3 books. Students should conclude that steeper ramps make rolling objects move faster than gentler ramps.

ENGAGE

Tap Prior Knowledge

- Ask student to think about the different ways they have learned that people can change motion. Remind students of the soccer players using hard and soft pushes to move balls, the people using weak and strong pulls to move a sled, the football players starting and stopping a ball, and the tennis and hockey players changing the direction of moving objects. Have students share the different ways they were able to change the way objects moved during their previous investigations.

EXPLORE

- Have students wear safety goggles.
- Guide students through the investigation. Read aloud pages 24–25 together.

My science notebook Help students make a table for recording their observations in their science notebook.

Example:

Changing Speed

Size of Ramp	What I Predict	Speed of Car
1 book		
3 books		

- Show students the materials they will be using, having students match each pictured item to the real item as they say the object's name.
- Read aloud the heading, and then the investigation question: *How can you change the speed of an object?* Read aloud the steps on page 25. Tell students that they will follow these steps to answer the question. Move from group to group and clarify steps if necessary.

- Have students make predictions of what might happen to the toy car during the investigation. During steps 1 and 3, remind students that they want to make their ramp stable. Stress that the goal is to release the car from the top of the ramp, not to push the car down the ramp.
- For steps 2 and 4, ask: **What did you observe about the speed of the car as it rolled down the ramp?** Remind students to record their observations for each ramp size in their tables. Encourage students to use pictures and words to describe what they observed.
- Have students in each group discuss their findings amongst themselves. Encourage comparisons, asking probing questions such as: **On which ramp did the car travel faster? Slower?**

EXPLAIN

- Have each group review their predictions and compare them with what happened. Guide students to review the observations recorded in their tables and use them to explain their results. Ask: **What was different about the way the car rolled down the 1-book ramp versus the 3-book ramp?** (The taller ramp made the car travel faster than the shorter ramp.) **Why do you think the car's speed was different for each ramp?** (Objects roll faster down steeper ramps than lower ramps.) **How can you change the speed of the car?** (I can use steeper or lower ramps to make the car roll faster or slower.)
- As each group shares explanations and conclusions, encourage students to ask questions to increase understanding. Students should listen for other interpretations and ideas. Discuss possible reasons for any differences in results or explanations.

ELABORATE

- Have groups continue the investigation to further support their conclusions. Provide additional books for students to make taller ramps (up to 5 books). Encourage groups to predict what will happen to the speed of the car when allowed to roll down steeper ramps.
- Have students record their results in their science notebook. Revisit students' conclusions from the original investigation. Ask: **Did the car roll faster or slower down a ramp made with 5 books or down a ramp made with 3 books?** Encourage students to discuss how their results support their conclusions from the original investigation.

EVALUATE

My science notebook

Have students record their answer to the Wrap It Up question in their science notebook.

Wrap It Up!

1. EXPLAIN **How did the speed of the toy car change?** (The toy car moved faster down the ramp made with 3 books than the ramp made with 1 book. The speed got faster as I made my ramp taller.)

READING CONNECTION

Describe the Relationship

With prompting and support, describe the relationship between illustrations and the text in which they appear (e.g., what person, place, thing, or idea in the text an illustration depicts).

As you begin the EXPLORE section, remind students what a ramp is, and that they have used ramps in previous *Investigate* activities. Then direct students to step 1. Point out the word *ramp* and the accompanying picture. Ask a volunteer to use the information in step 1 (both picture instructions) to explain what they are to do to construct the ramp. Then have students find other places where the word *ramp* is used in the steps. Say: **Use the pictures and the text to describe how the ramp you will make in step 3 is different from the one you will make in step 1.** (The ramp in step 3 has three books; the ramp in step 1 has one book.)

Plan and Conduct an Investigation

NEXT GENERATION SCIENCE STANDARDS | PERFORMANCE EXPECTATION

K-PS2-1: Plan and conduct an investigation to compare the effects of different strengths or different directions of pushes and pulls on the motion of an object. [Clarification Statement: Examples of pushes or pulls could include a string attached to an object being pulled, a person pushing an object, a person stopping a rolling ball, and two objects colliding and pushing on each other.] *[Assessment Boundary: Assessment is limited to different relative strengths or different directions, but not both at the same time. Assessment does not include non-contact pushes or pulls such as those produced by magnets.]*

Objective Students will be able to:

- Plan and conduct an investigation to compare the effects of different strengths or different directions of pushes and pulls on the motion of an object.

CLASSROOM MANAGEMENT

Suggested Materials ***For groups of 4:*** Provide a variety of materials for students to choose from, including balls; blocks; toy cars; string; tape; paper or plastic cups; writing and drawing materials such as pencils, colored pencils, crayons, markers

Time 10 minutes for planning each test; 10 minutes for testing each plan; 10 minutes for recording results of each test; 5 minutes for comparisons

Teaching Tips In order to fulfill the performance expectations, students must choose their own materials and plan and conduct an investigation to compare how different strengths or directions of pushes and pulls affect the motion of an object. Encourage students to choose an object that they can both push and pull. Remind students that they can attach a string to their object, if necessary, to test pulling it. Model lab safety by wearing your safety goggles.

What to Expect Students will observe that their objects will move at different speeds and distances depending upon the strength of the pushes or pulls applied. Strong pushes or pulls will make their objects travel faster and farther. Weak pushes or pulls will make their objects travel slower and not as far. Students will also observe that they can use pushes and pulls from different directions to make their objects move in varying ways. A push will always move objects away from the "pusher." For example, a push from the left will make an object move right; a push from the back will make an object move forward; and so on. A pull will always move objects toward the "puller." For example, a pull from the left will move an object left; a pull from the back will move an object back; and so on.

ENGAGE

Set the scene.

- Talk with students about the different ways that they can move objects using their hands and feet. Review some of the different ball games that students explored in previous lessons. Ask: **What can you do to move a ball?** (Students may say that they can throw it, roll it, or kick it.) Remind students that throwing, rolling, and kicking are all types of pushes. Ask: **What can you do to move a wagon?** (Students may say that they can pull it or push it with a handle.)
- Direct students to look at the picture of the bobsled team on page 27. Say: **These men are pushing a bobsled. They are trying to make the sled move as quickly as possible.** Discuss that the people on the team run as quickly as they can while pushing the sled in order to get the sled moving at a very fast speed. Then they jump into the sled and ride it down a steep track.

Plan an investigation.

My science notebook

Tell students that they will plan and conduct their own investigation to answer the following question: *How can you use pushes and pulls to make things move?*

Make it clear that students are not guessing an answer to the question at this time. They will plan and carry out the investigation to answer the question.

- Read the steps on pages 26–27 aloud, pointing out that students will perform two different explorations in order to answer the main question. The first test will use hard and soft pushes and pulls to make objects move. The second test will use pushes and pulls from different directions to make objects move.
- Guide students as they plan their investigations by asking the following questions:
  - **Which object will you choose for your tests?**
  - **What will you use to push your object?**
  - **What will you use to pull your object?**
  - **In which directions will you push and pull your object?**

Have students agree upon a plan with the members of their group. Help students draw their ideas and record their plans in their science notebook. Example: We chose to use a toy car for our investigations. We plan to move the car with our hands using hard and soft pushes. We plan to move the car with a string using strong and weak pulls. We will try to move the car by pushing and pulling it from the back, the front, the left, and the right.

- Have students make a table for recording their observations.
  Example:

Making Things Move

Type of Push or Pull	What I Predict	How the Object Moved
hard push		
soft push		
strong pull		
weak pull		
push from left		
push from right		
pull from left		
pull from right		

SCIENCE AND ENGINEERING PRACTICES

Planning and Carrying Out Investigations

- Discuss with students how often scientists plan and conduct their investigations together to produce data that will give the scientists the evidence they need to answer a question. Encourage students to collaborate, or work as a group, to build their own objects, and using the data they collected, refine their object design to move in the way they wish.

Connections to Nature of Science
Scientific Investigations Use a Variety of Methods

- Discuss with students how scientists use different ways to study the world. Encourage students to identify some ways that they can learn about the world around them.

CROSSCUTTING CONCEPTS

Cause and Effect

- Remind students that in this investigation they tested a cause and effect relationship - a bigger push caused faster movements in their objects (the effect). Tell students that identifying cause and effect relationships is a fundamental part of being a scientist. Ask: **What are other cause and effect relationships you can think of in your own lives?** (accept reasonable answers). Have students verbally identify what the cause and effect is in each situation.

Plan and Conduct an Investigation (continued)

EXPLORE

Conduct an investigation.

- Have students wear safety goggles.
- Have students test their ideas to answer the questions in steps 2 and 5, first testing their ideas about hard and soft pushes and pulls, and then testing their ideas about pushes and pulls from different directions.
- Ask students questions to foster thorough observations:
  - **How did your object move when you gave it a hard push? A soft push?**
  - **What happened to your object when you pushed it from different directions? Pulled it from different directions?**
  - **What made your object move toward you? Away from you?**
- Guide students to pay close attention to the speed, distance, and direction that their object travels in each test. Have students record the results of each test in their science notebook.

EXPLAIN

Review your results.

- Have groups review the results of their tests. Then reread step 7 and have groups compare how using different pushes and pulls moved their object. Help students explain these comparisons. Ask:
  - **What made your object move the fastest? The slowest?**
  - **Which type of push or pull made your object move the farthest?**
  - **What was the best way to move your object forward? Backward?**
- Revisit the question from the beginning of the investigation: *How can you use pushes and pulls to make things move?* Ask: **How can you use your results to answer the question?** Help students draw conclusions about the different ways they can make objects move. Ask:
  - **Why do strong pushes and pulls move objects differently than soft pushes and pulls?**
  - **How does pushing and pulling from different directions make objects move?** Example explanation: The toy car moved every time we pushed or pulled it. Pushes made the car move away from us. Pulls made the car move toward us. We used hard and soft pushes and pulls to move the toy car. It moved the farthest and fastest when we used hard pushes and pulls. It moved slower and not as far when we used soft pushes and pulls. When we pushed and pulled the car from the left and right sides, it moved, but not very far. When we pushed and pulled the car from the back and the front, it moved better and farther because it could roll on its wheels. When we pushed the car, it always moved away from us in the same direction we pushed it. When we pulled the car, it followed us.

Share your results.

- Have groups use their data to share their observations and conclusions with the class. Encourage students to explain what their results show, and on what evidence they based their conclusions.
- Ask: **In what ways did you think like a scientist as you completed this activity?** (Possible answer: I worked with my partner to carry out an investigation. We picked objects to test, and recorded our data in our notebooks. We compared our drawings afterwards to see how strong and weak pushes and pulls affect different objects.)

ELABORATE

Have students perform the investigation again using a different classroom object. If a group chose to use an object with wheels, encourage them to choose an object without wheels this time and visa versa. Direct students to follow the same steps they followed before, while also using the same plan and table for recording their results.

- Remind students to use the same strength pushes and pulls as they did previously and to also push and pull their new object in the same directions as they did previously. Once groups have completed this second investigation, ask: **Did the results of this investigation support your original results?** Encourage groups to share their results and conclusions.

EVALUATE

Check to make sure students organized their data into the table in their science notebook and recorded their conclusions. Then ask students these questions. Have them record the answers in their science notebook.

1. **COMPARE AND CONTRAST** **What was the same about using hard and soft pushes to make your object move? What was different?** (Each time we pushed our object, it moved away from us. When we used a hard push, the object moved faster and farther than when we used a soft push.)
2. **APPLY** **How can you make objects move forward?** (I can push an object from the back to make it move forward. I can pull an object from the front to make it move forward.)
3. **INFER** **What would happen if you gave a ball a strong push at one end of a table?** (The ball would roll away from me and across the table. The ball might keep moving and roll off the other end of the table.)

RUBRICS

Teacher Rubric Use the scale descriptions to guide your assessment of the student's work. Assess each item separately, and then decide on one overall score, using the following scale:

4: Student performs with thorough understanding.
3: Student performs with adequate understanding.
2: Student performs with basic understanding.
1: Student performs with limited understanding.

Rubric	Scale			
The student planned and conducted an investigation.	4	3	2	1
The student's investigation produced data that could be organized in a table.	4	3	2	1
The student analyzed data recorded in the table and used them as the basis for drawing conclusions from evidence to answer the questions.	4	3	2	1
The student made comparisons using the data and communicated the plan, the results, and conclusions to others.	4	3	2	1
Overall Score				

Student Rubric Have students complete a self-evaluation similar to that shown below.

Rubric	Yes	Not Yet
1. I can plan an investigation and carry out the steps.		
2. I can gather data and organize my findings.		
3. I can analyze my results and draw a conclusion from them.		
4. I can explain what I did, what happened, and what I learned from my investigation.		

NATIONAL GEOGRAPHIC LEARNING | Think Like an Engineer

Analyze Data

NEXT GENERATION SCIENCE STANDARDS | DISCIPLINARY CORE IDEAS

ETS1.A: Defining Engineering Problems A situation that people want to change or create can be approached as a problem to be solved through engineering. Such problems may have many acceptable solutions. (secondary to K-PS2-2)

NEXT GENERATION SCIENCE STANDARDS | PERFORMANCE EXPECTATION

K-PS2-2. Analyze data to determine if a design solution works as intended to change the speed or direction of an object with a push or a pull. [Clarification Statement: Examples of problems requiring a solution could include having a marble or other object move a certain distance, follow a particular path, and knock down other objects. Examples of solutions could include tools such as a ramp to increase the speed of the object and a structure that would cause an object such as a marble or ball to turn.] *[Assessment Boundary: Assessment does not include friction as a mechanism for change in speed.]*

K-2-ETS1-1. Ask questions, make observations, and gather information about a situation people want to change to define a simple problem that can be solved through the development of a new or improved object or tool.

Objective **Students will be able to:**

- Analyze data to determine if a design solution works as intended to change the speed or direction of an object with a push or a pull.

CLASSROOM MANAGEMENT

Suggested Materials ***For groups of 4:*** one marble; 3 small paper cups; a variety of other materials from which students can choose, including: pieces of cardboard; boards and books for making ramps; cardboard boxes; construction paper; string or yarn; cardboard tubes; pipe insulation that has been cut in half lengthwise to form a track; plastic bottles; rubber bands; chenille sticks; markers; scissors; tape

Time 10 minutes for planning; 15 minutes for drawing and building; 10 minutes for testing and recording; 10 minutes for analysis and redesign, if needed; 10 minutes for sharing

Advance Preparation Collect and assemble all of the materials where students can see and use them. Provide a place for each group to test their design, whether groups have separate locations on the floor, or separate tables if floor space is not plausible.

Teaching Tips Student groups should design their prototypes and conduct their tests by themselves. Coach students through the planning process without instructing them on specific steps to take or materials to use. Facilitate the building of designs by providing cutting and taping support, as needed. Model lab safety by wearing your safety goggles.

What to Expect Students will observe that when tested, their plans allow for one marble to roll across the floor, change direction, and knock down a collection of paper cups. Some groups may find that their first plan does not provide enough speed for the marble to roll, collide, change direction, and knock down cups, or that the end target of cups is not achieved. Groups may need to adjust plans as needed to achieve their goals.

ENGAGE

Set the scene.

- Read the heading and introductory text on page 28. Say: **In this lesson you will analyze data. Data are pieces of information that you collect. When you analyze the information, you are taking a close look at the information to see what you can learn from it.** Discuss with students that they analyze information every day when they think about things, look closely at them, and draw conclusions from what they have learned.
- Direct students to look at the picture of the marbles on page 29. Explain that in this lesson, students will be planning, or designing, ways to make a marble move in different ways, analyzing their plan, and making changes as needed.

Define a problem.

- Read aloud the problem under step 1: *How can you make a marble roll across the floor, change direction, and knock down some cups?* Make it clear that students will not be guessing an answer to the problem at this time. Instead, they will be designing and testing a way to make a marble move in the ways described.

EXPLORE

Make a plan.

Read step 2 together. Guide students as they make their plan and draw a picture of it, asking the following questions:

- **How can you start the marble rolling?**
- **Do you want your marble to move quickly or slowly?**
- **What makes a moving object change its direction?**
- **What materials can you use to make the marble change direction?**
- **What does the marble need to do to knock down the cups?**

- After students have agreed upon a plan with the members of their group, have group members draw a picture of their idea in their science notebook. Encourage students to include as many details as they can in their drawings. Assist students with writing words or a sentence describing their pictures/ideas. Examples of student ideas may include using blocks or tubes as a ramp to start the marble rolling quickly, using books or blocks as obstacles into which the marble will collide and change direction, and setting 1–3 paper

SCIENCE AND ENGINEERING PRACTICES

Analyze and Interpreting Data

- Discuss with students how scientists often test their tools to make sure they are working properly. One way they can do this is by using the tool for the job it's meant to do and observing how well it performs. Remind students that they will be testing their tools in this investigations. If they find their tools are not working the way they expected, they can revise or change the way their tools are set up. Students can change the design of their ramp to best move the marble. Ask: **How will you know if you need to change the design of your ramp?** (Possible answer: the marble does not roll to the end of the ramp.) Ask: **What kind of observations will you make?** (I will observer how far the marble travels.) Ask: **What kind of data will you collect?** (I will collect data on how far and in what direction the marble moves.) Then ask: **Based on your observations, what kinds of data would help you identify problems in your design?** (Possible answer: If the marble does not roll all the way down the ramp, I would know that there is a problem with the ramp.)

Asking Questions and Defining Problems

- Discuss with students how scientists ask questions based on their observations of the world around them. Often, after a problem is identified, scientists design a solution to that problem. Have students identify a problem or need related to their lives. Encourage students to design a solution to that problem in their science notebook and discuss their solution with their classmates.

CROSSCUTTING CONCEPTS

Cause and Effect

- Discuss with students how scientists use simple tests to gather evidence. Explain that this evidence can be used to support or refute other scientists' ideas about causes and effects of an issue. Ask: **What types of changes did you make to the design of your ramp to make the moving object change direction?** (Possible answer: I attached another ramp to the original and turned it a different direction.) Ask: **If your classmate told you that the moving object would not change direction with the design change you made, how could you gather evidence and test what he or she told you?** (Possible answer: I could roll the object down the ramp and show evidence of the change in direction.)

Analyze Data (continued)

EXPLORE (continued)

cups at a location matching the path that the marble will take after changing direction.

Test your idea.

Read steps 3 and 4 together. Guide students in carrying out a fair test and recording their results. Students may wish to test their idea several times to observe and record what happens each time.

Record your results.

- Discuss with students ways in which they can record their results. Point out that scientists often use tables to help them organize their data. Help them make a data table in their science notebook. An example is shown below. Example:

Making Marbles Move

Test	Roll Across the Floor	Change Direction	Knock Over Cups
trial 1			
trial 2			
trial 3			

EXPLAIN

Refine your idea.

- Read aloud step 5 together. Remind students that the results they have recorded are data. When they look at their data and think about what they mean, they are analyzing their data. Analyzing data prepares them to answer the question they have been investigating.
- Remind students of the problem they were working to solve: *How can you make a marble roll across the floor, change directions, and knock down some cups?* Help them in analyzing their results in light of this question. Ask:
  - **What are your results? Did your plan work?**
  - **Did your plan make the marble roll across the floor, change directions, and knock down some cups?**
  - **If not, how will you change your plan to work better?**
- Encourage students to change their designs if the marble is not rolling, changing direction, and knocking down cups well with their first design. After modifications are made, students should perform the test again, recording their results in another table in their science notebook.
- When students are satisfied with their results, revisit the question again: *How can you make a marble roll across the floor, change directions, and knock down some cups?* Ask: **How can you use your results to answer the question?** Have students use evidence from their data to support their answers to the question.

<u>Example of student conclusions:</u> Our group planned to use a ramp made of a block and a piece of wood to start the marble rolling quickly into a cardboard tube, which led to a hardcover book standing on its side. At the end of the path we placed 2 small cups side-by-side. When we started our marble, it rolled down the ramp, through the tube and collided with the book, making the marble turn left and move toward the cups. The marble did not reach the cups. We changed our plan, moving the cups closer to the book, one in front of the other, and making the ramp steeper using two stacked blocks under the board. When we tried the marble on our new design plan, it rolled, hit the book, changed direction, and knocked down one of the cups. We concluded that we needed to make the marble move really fast to roll, change direction, and knock down both cups. We also concluded that even though the marble knocked down only 1 cup, it could probably knock down both if the cups were moved a bit.

Share your solution.

- Have groups use their tables and drawings to share their ideas and results with the class. Encourage them to use the data from their investigations to support their ideas. Allow students to ask questions and make suggestions for improvements.
- Ask: **In what ways did you think like an engineer as you completed this activity?** (Possible answers: I thought of different ways to

make my marble move. I tried different tests on my design, such as rolling it over the floor, changing direction, and knocking down cups. I looked at my results and decided how well each design worked.)

ELABORATE

- Extend the investigation by having groups make a new plan using different materials to make the marble roll and change direction. Encourage students to use any feedback they received from classmates during the sharing process as they plan their new designs. Have students follow the same steps as before, using a variety of materials, conducting tests, and recording results in a table. Allow time for students to present their plans, results, and conclusions to the class.

EVALUATE

My science notebook Check to make sure that students have recorded their plans, data, and conclusions in their science notebook. Then ask students these questions. Have them record the answers in their science notebook.

1. **EXPLAIN How can you make a moving marble change direction?** (I can make the marble hit something, such as a book, box, or the wall. When the marble hits the object, it pushes against it and moves away from it. It changes direction.) Some students may have used the pipe insulation tube to make a curve that their marble followed, changing direction in the process.
2. **INFER What might happen to the cups if the marble is not moving quickly?** (Sample answers: The marble may not roll far enough to hit the cups. The marble may just tap the cups without knocking them over.)
3. **MAKE JUDGEMENTS Why is a marble a good object to use to test motion?** (Marbles roll easily. They are small and can move fast. They are not very heavy. They work well rolling on the floor, over and through things, and can be started and stopped easily.)

RUBRICS

Teacher Rubric Use the scale descriptions to guide your assessment of the student's work. Assess each item separately, and then decide on one overall score, using the following scale:

4: Student performs with thorough understanding.
3: Student performs with adequate understanding.
2: Student performs with basic understanding.
1: Student performs with limited understanding.

Rubric	Scale			
The student planned an investigation to solve this problem: *How can you make a marble roll across the floor, change directions, and knock down some cups?*	4	3	2	1
The student followed a plan to make a marble move as described in the problem statement.	4	3	2	1
The student made observations to collect data that could be used to make comparisons. The student organized their observations in a table.	4	3	2	1
The student analyzed the data and drew conclusions about the effectiveness of the plan.	4	3	2	1
The student revised their plan based on observations, and tested again.	4	3	2	1
The student used evidence from the activity to clearly communicated the plan, data, analysis, and revision to others.	4	3	2	1
Overall Score				

Student Rubric Have students complete a self-evaluation similar to that shown below.

Rubric	Yes	Not Yet
1. I can plan an investigation to solve a problem.		
2. I can carry out an investigation, following my plan.		
3. I can gather data and organize my findings.		
4. I can analyze the data I collect and draw a conclusion based on evidence.		
5. I can change my plan to make it work better.		
6. I can explain what I did and what I found out to others, using evidence from my investigation to support my conclusions.		

Pilot

NEXT GENERATION SCIENCE STANDARDS | CONNECTION TO NATURE OF SCIENCE
Scientific Investigations Use a Variety of Methods Scientists use different ways to study the world.

Objective Students will be able to:
- Connect concepts about forces and motion with the career of pilot.

ENGAGE

Tap Prior Knowledge

- Invite students to discuss any experiences they have had with airplanes, whether students have flown on one, seen one flying in the sky, or seen an airplane in flight in a movie or on television. Say: **Airplanes move from one place to another by flying in the air.** Ask: **Do you have any ideas about what makes an airplane move?** Have students share their ideas. Discuss why people might travel in an airplane. Students may suggest that people fly to get somewhere, to go on a trip or vacation, or to visit someone.

EXPLORE

Explore Airplanes

- Show page 30 to students. Ask: **What do you see in this picture? Why do you think the man is in front of the airplane?**
- Have students share their answers. Students may say that they see an airplane and a man squatting in front of it. Some students may suggest that the man flies the airplane or works with airplanes.

Set a Purpose and Read

- Tell students to listen to find out about a pilot who is a National Geographic Explorer.
- Have students listen as you read aloud page 30.

EXPLAIN

Describe the Work of an Explorer Who Is a Pilot

- Reread aloud again page 30. Say: **Barrington Irving is a National Geographic Explorer.** Explain that an explorer is someone who travels to different places around the world to experience new things, meet different people, and learn about new places. Explorers search for information and study people, places, and things for a long time. Say: **Barrington Irving was the youngest person to fly alone around the world**. Discuss how flying around the world would take a very long time. If possible, show students a globe so that they can see the distance it would take to travel around it. Explain that airplanes usually fly to one location and stop, refuel, and then return home.
- Point to the picture of Barrington Irving on page 30. Ask: **What does Barrington Irving do?** (He is a pilot.) Explain that a pilot is a person who controls the airplane as it takes off, flies, and lands. Say: **People go to school to learn things. People can go to a special school to learn how to drive a car. Barrington Irving went to a special school to learn about airplanes, what makes them move, and how to fly them.** Explain that Barrington Irving travels all around the world in his airplane. Then he shares what he learns with others. Ask: **How does Barrington Irving share what he has learned about airplanes and flying?** (He teaches children about science and technology.)

Connect Science Topics to the Work of a Pilot

- Say: **We have been learning about making things move.** Direct students to look at the picture of the airplane on page 30. Ask: **What do you think might happen when Barrington Irving starts the engine of this airplane?** (The airplane will move; the propellers will start spinning; the airplane will take off and fly in the sky.) **In what direction will the airplane move?** (forward) **What helps the airplane move?** (The propellers spin very fast; the wheels help it roll down the runway.) **Do you think airplanes move slowly or quickly?** (quickly)
- Ask: **Why do you think Barrington Irving needs to understand motion?** (He is a pilot; he flies airplanes and makes them move in different ways to travel around the world.)

Find Out More

- Ask: **Is a pilot's job interesting to you? Why or why not?** (Allow students to share their answers. Accept all positive and negative responses.) For students who find this to be an interesting career, ask: **Why would you like to be a pilot?** (Possible answer: I would like to be a pilot because I would like to fly to far-away places.)

ELABORATE

Find Out More About Airplanes

My science notebook

Help students explore different magazines and Internet resources to find pictures of different types of airplanes. Discuss how airplanes are used for all different types of travel. Some carry passengers. Others carry cargo. Some are used to help people in danger. Explain that the airplane pictured with Barrington Irving uses a propeller to move, and that some airplanes use jet engines instead of propellers to push the airplane forward. Invite students to print or cut out pictures of the different airplanes they find and place them in their science notebook.

EVALUATE

My science notebook

Ask students these questions. Have them record their answers in their science notebook.

1. **RECALL** **What did Barrington Irving do at age 23?** (He become the youngest person to fly alone around the world.)
2. **APPLY** **Why does a pilot need to understand motion?** (Airplanes move in the air and on the ground. Pilots drive and fly airplanes. So pilots need to understand how to stop and start the airplane, and how to keep the airplane in motion while flying in the air.)

READING CONNECTION

Retell Key Details

With prompting and support, identify the main topic and retell key details of a text.

Guide students in retelling key details of this science career feature. For example, in the EXPLAIN section when asking students to describe the work of an explorer, have students identify that Barrington Irving's work as a pilot and teacher allows him to travel around the world and then share what he has learned with others. Also in the EXPLAIN section when asking students to connect science topics to the work of an pilot, have students identify that Barrington Irving needed to learn about the science of motion in order to do his job and to teach others.

Test Administration Script for DCI Review: Physical Science

For Questions 1–10

SAY: You are going to take a short test about pushes and pulls. Listen to the directions. (Hold up a page and point.) For each question, you will look at the pictures and listen to a question. Then you will circle one picture to mark your answer. Before you start, are there any questions? (Pause.)

1. Find number 1. Circle the picture that shows a push. (PS2.A)
2. Find number 2. Circle the picture that shows a pull. (PS2.A)
3. Find number 3. Circle the picture that shows a push that will put an object into motion. (PS2.A)
4. Find number 4. Circle the picture that shows a person using a pull. (PS2.A)
5. Find number 5. Circle the picture that shows two objects that will hit each other, causing one object to quickly change speed and direction. (PS2.B)
6. Find number 6. Circle the picture that shows how a big push can make something speed up quickly. (PS3.C)
7. Find number 7. Circle the picture that shows someone using a strong pull to change the direction of motion. (PS2.A)
8. Find number 8. Circle the picture that shows a person using a big push to make something move quickly. (PS3.C)
9. Find number 9. Circle the picture that shows the object that needs the hardest push to put it into motion. (PS2.A)
10. Find number 10. Circle the picture that shows two objects that will push on each other, causing one object to quickly change speed and direction. (PS2.B)

Name ______________________________

DCI Review: Physical Science

1

A

B

C

2

A

B

C

3

A

B

C

4

A

B

C

Name ____

5

A

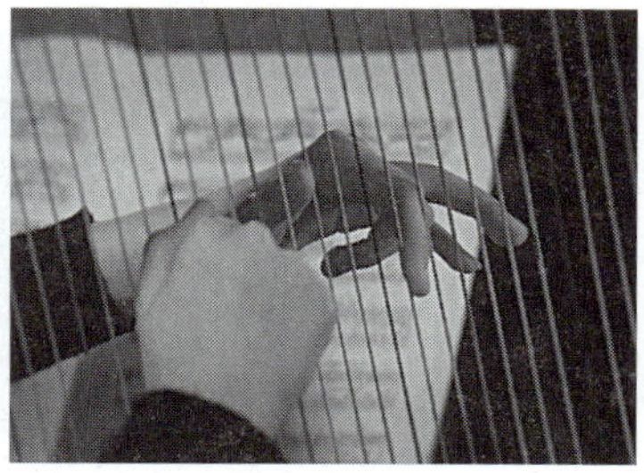

B

C

6

A

B

C

7

A

B

C

Name ______________________________

8

A

B

C

9

A

B

C

10

A

B

C

Pauta para tomar la prueba para el repaso de las IDB: Ciencias físicas

Para las preguntas 1 a 10

DIGA: Van a dar una prueba corta sobre empujar y jalar. Escuchen las instrucciones. (Muestre una página y señálela). Para cada pregunta, mirarán los dibujos y escucharán una pregunta. Luego, encerrarán su respuesta en un círculo. Antes de comenzar, ¿tienen alguna duda? (Haga una pausa).

1. Hallen el número 1. Encierren en un círculo el dibujo que muestra cómo empujar. (PS2.A)

2. Hallen el número 2. Encierren en un círculo el dibujo que muestra cómo jalar. (PS2.A)

3. Hallen el número 3. Encierren en un círculo el dibujo que muestra que empujar un objeto hará que este comience a moverse. (PS2.A)

4. Hallen el número 4. Encierren en un círculo el dibujo que muestra que una persona jala algo para cambiar su movimiento. (PS2.A)

5. Hallen el número 5. Encierren en un círculo el dibujo que muestra dos objetos que chocarán, cambiando su dirección y velocidad. (PS2.B)

6. Hallen el número 6. Encierren en un círculo el dibujo que muestra que empujar con fuerza puede hacer que algo acelere rápidamente. (PS3.C)

7. Hallen el número 7. Encierren en un círculo el dibujo que muestra a una persona que jala con fuerza para cambiar la dirección del movimiento. (PS2.A)

8. Hallen el número 8. Encierren en un círculo el dibujo que muestra a una persona que empuja con fuerza para hacer que algo se mueva rápidamente. (PS3.C)

9. Hallen el número 9. Encierren en un círculo el dibujo que muestra el objeto que necesita el empuje más fuerte para comenzar a moverse. (PS2.A)

10. Hallen el número 10. Encierren en un círculo el dibujo que muestra dos objetos que se empujarán entre sí y harán que un objeto cambie de dirección. (PS2.B)

Nombre ____________________

Repaso de las IDB: Ciencias físicas

1

A

B

C

2

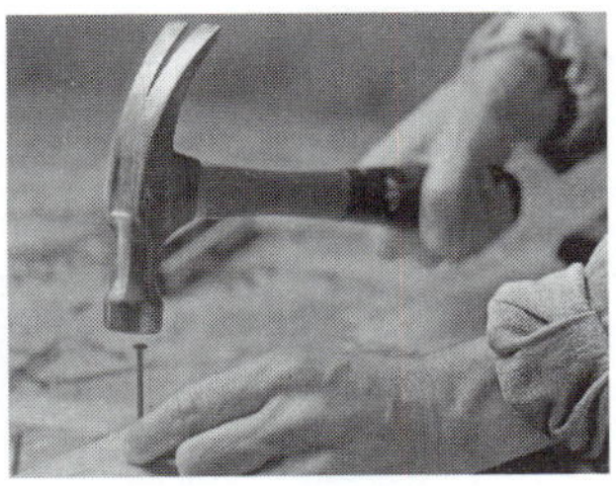

A

B

C

3

A

B

C

4

A

B

C

Nombre ______________________________

5

A

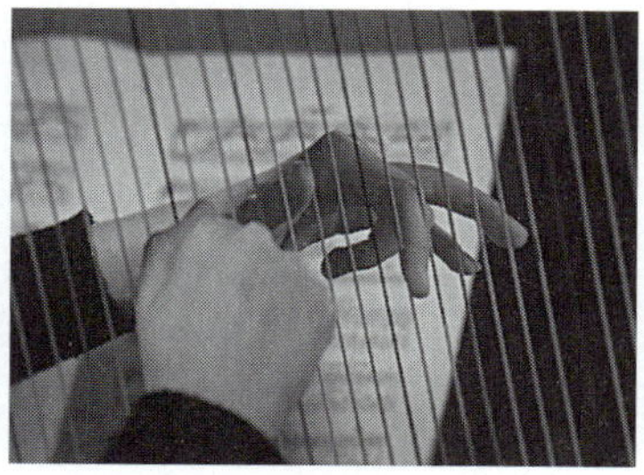

B

C

6

A

B

C

7

A

B

C

Nombre ______________________________

8

A

B

C

9

A

B

C

10

A

B

C

DCI Review Answer Key for Physical Science

PHYSICAL SCIENCE

K. Forces and Interactions: Pushes and Pulls

Question Number	Answer
1	B
2	B
3	A
4	C
5	A
6	C
7	B
8	B
9	A
10	C

NOTES

Life Science

Grade K. Interdependent Relationships in Ecosystems: Animals, Plants, and Their Environment

Performance Expectations

Students who demonstrate understanding can:

K-LS1-1. Use observations to describe patterns of what plants and animals (including humans) need to survive. [Clarification Statement: Examples of patterns could include that animals need to take in food but plants do not; the different kinds of food needed by different types of animals; the requirement of plants to have light; and that all living things need water.]

K-ESS2-2. Construct an argument supported by evidence for how plants and animals (including humans) can change the environment to meet their needs. [Clarification Statement: Examples of plants and animals changing their environment could include a squirrel digs in the ground to hide its food and tree roots can break concrete.]

K-ESS3-1. Use a model to represent the relationship between the needs of different plants or animals (including humans) and the places they live. [Clarification Statement: Examples of relationships could include that deer eat buds and leaves, therefore, they usually live in forested areas, and grasses need sunlight so they often grow in meadows. Plants, animals, and their surroundings make up a system.]

K-ESS3-3. Communicate solutions that will reduce the impact of humans on the land, water, air, and/or other living things in the local environment. [Clarification Statement: Examples of human impact on the land could include cutting trees to produce paper and using resources to produce bottles. Examples of solutions could include reusing paper and recycling cans and bottles.]

Disciplinary Core Ideas

LS1.C: Organization for Matter and Energy Flow in Organisms

- All animals need food in order to live and grow. They obtain their food from plants or from other animals. Plants need water and light to live and grow. (K-LS1-1)

ESS2.E: Biogeology

- Plants and animals can change their environment. (K-ESS2-2)

ESS3.A: Natural Resources

- Living things need water, air, and resources from the land, and they live in places that have the things they need. Humans use natural resources for everything they do. (K-ESS3-1)

ESS3.C: Human Impacts on Earth Systems

- Things that people do to live comfortably can affect the world around them. But they can make choices that reduce their impacts on the land, water, air, and other living things. *(secondary to K-ESS2-2)*, (K-ESS3-3)

ETS1.B: Developing Possible Solutions

- Designs can be conveyed through sketches, drawings, or physical models. These representations are useful in communicating ideas for a problem's solutions to other people. *(secondary to K-ESS3-3)*

Science and Engineering Practices

Analyzing and Interpreting Data

Analyzing data in K–2 builds on prior experiences and progresses to collecting, recording, and sharing observations.

- Use observations (firsthand or from media) to describe patterns in the natural world in order to answer scientific questions. (K-LS1-1)

Engaging in Argument from Evidence

Engaging in argument from evidence in K–2 builds on prior experiences and progresses to comparing ideas and representations about the natural and designed world(s).

- Construct an argument with evidence to support a claim. (K-ESS2-2)

Developing and Using Models

Analyzing Modeling in K–2 builds on prior experiences and progresses to include using and developing models (i.e., diagram, drawing, physical replica, diorama, dramatization, storyboard) that represent concrete events or design solutions.

- Use a model to represent relationships in the natural world. (K-ESS3-1)

Obtaining, Evaluating, and Communicating Information

Obtaining, evaluating, and communicating information in K–2 builds on prior experiences and uses observations and texts to communicate new information.

- Communicate solutions with others in oral and/or written forms using models and/or drawings that provide detail about scientific ideas. (K-ESS3-3)

Connections to Nature of Science

Scientific Knowledge is Based on Empirical Evidence

- Scientists look for patterns and order when making observations about the world. (K-LS1-1)

Crosscutting Concepts

Patterns

- Patterns in the natural and human designed world can be observed and used as evidence. (K-LS1-1)

Systems and System Models

- Systems in the natural and designed world have parts that work together. (K-ESS2-2), (K-ESS3-1)

Cause and Effect

Events have causes that generate observable patterns. (K-ESS3-3)

K-2-ETS1 Engineering Design

Performance Expectations

K-2-ETS1-2. Develop a simple sketch, drawing, or physical model to illustrate how the shape of an object helps it function as needed to solve a given problem.

Science and Engineering Practices

Developing and Using Models

Modeling in K–2 builds on prior experiences and progresses to include using and developing models (i.e., diagram, drawing, physical replica, diorama, dramatization, or storyboard) that represent concrete events or design solutions.

- Develop a simple model based on evidence to represent a proposed object or tool. (K-2-ETS1-2)

Crosscutting Concepts

Structure and Function

- The shape and stability of structures of natural and designed objects are related to their function(s). (K-2-ETS1-2)

Living Things

NEXT GENERATION SCIENCE STANDARDS | DISCIPLINARY CORE IDEAS

ESS3.A: Natural Resources Living things need water, air, and resources from the land, and they live in places that have the things they need. (K-ESS3-1)

Objectives **Students will be able to:**

- Define *living*.
- Explain that living things are alive and they grow and change.

Science Vocabulary

living

ENGAGE

Tap Prior Knowledge

- Have one volunteer stand up in front of the class. Ask: **Does [student's name] grow and change?** (Yes.) **Is [student's name] alive?** (Yes.) Say: **[Student's name] is living because [he/she] is alive and [he/she] grows and changes.**
- Discuss other living things that students know, such as friends, family, pets, plants, and other animals.

EXPLORE

Preview the Lesson

- Show pages 4–5, and have students take a picture walk with you. Have students share what they see in the woodland scene. Direct students to notice different living things, such as the bear and different plants. Ask: **What is the bear doing?**
- Have students share their answers. Students may say that the bear is standing on rocks looking at the water. Students may say that the bear is looking for something in the water or getting ready to take a drink of water.

Set a Purpose and Read

- Read the main heading. Tell students to listen to find out about living things and what they need.
- Have students follow along as you read pages 4–5.

EXPLAIN

Define Living

- Direct students to revisit the picture on pages 4–5. Reread the heading and text aloud, pointing to the word *living* each time it is read. Point to the bear and say: **The bear is alive. It grows and changes. The bear is a *living* thing. Nonliving things were never alive. They do not grow and change.**
- Point to different living and nonliving things in the picture, such as rocks, water, and different plants. Have students identify the object you are pointing to as living or not living. Encourage students to explain their answers using defining language. For example, point to the picture a rock and ask: **Is this rock a living thing?** (No.) **How do you know the rock is not a living thing?** (It does not grow or change. It is not alive.) **Is the water a living thing?** (No.) **How do you know the water is not a living thing?** (It is not alive and does not grow.) Point to a plant and ask: **Is this plant a living thing?** (Yes.) **How do you know the plant is a living thing?** (It grows and changes. It is alive.)
- Ask: **Aside from the bear, what other living things do you see?** (plants, including trees) Reinforce that the plants in the picture are also living things, even though they do not move around like the bear does.

ELABORATE

Find Out More About Bears

Help students find out about different kinds of bears (grizzly, brown, black, polar). The bear featured here is a white variant of the North American black bear, known as a Kermode bear. It is found in British Columbia. It may be white or cream in color, but it is not a polar bear, and lives in a forest habitat. Have students choose one type of bear. Provide books and Internet resources for students to use to explore their bear. Encourage students to find out where their bear lives (habitat), what it eats, and where it finds shelter. Have students draw a picture of the bear's habitat, food, and shelter in their science notebook. Help students to write descriptive words below their drawings as needed.

Extend Your Thinking About Living and Nonliving Things

Step 1: Remind students that living things grow and change. Explain that another word for a thing that is not living is *nonliving*. Have students take a walk around the playground or classroom to look for living and nonliving things. Have students share one living and one nonliving thing that they found with the class. Record answers on chart paper.

Step 2: If time allows, provide students with a clipboard, paper divided into two columns, and a pencil for them to use to record their findings as they explore. Have students draw a picture of an object in the left column, and in the right column place a check mark if the object is living or an "X" if the object is nonliving. Attach papers into their science notebook.

EVALUATE

Have students record their answers to the Wrap It Up questions in their science notebook.

Wrap It Up!

1. **IDENTIFY** **Name two living things.** (Students' answer will vary. Answers should include two living things.)

TEACHING WITH TECHNOLOGY

Identify Living and Nonliving Things

Project the lesson on a whiteboard. Invite a volunteer to point to one living thing. Have the students name the living thing. Ask: **Does this thing grow and change? Is it alive?** If the class answers *yes* to both questions, have the volunteer circle the living thing on the whiteboard. Repeat the exercise with a new volunteer, this time having the volunteer point to a nonliving thing. Ask: **Does it grow and change? Is it alive?** If the class answers *no* to both questions, have the volunteer draw an "X" over the nonliving thing on the whiteboard. Continue inviting volunteers to identify living and nonliving things, repeating the exercise of asking questions and marking the whiteboard accordingly each time.

READING CONNECTION

Understand Unknown Words

With prompting and support, ask and answer questions about unknown words in a text.

Guide students to ask and answer questions about unknown words in a text. For example, in the EXPLAIN section when asking students to identify living things in the picture, model this technique for students. Say: **As I look at each object in the picture, I ask myself, "Is it alive?" and "Does it grow and change?" If I answer, "Yes," then I know the object is a living thing. If I answer,"No," then I know it is not a living thing.** Have student practice this technique in the ELABORATE section when asking students to find both living and nonliving things.

Plants Are Living Things

NEXT GENERATION SCIENCE STANDARDS | DISCIPLINARY CORE IDEAS

ESS3.A: Natural Resources Living things need water, air, and resources from the land, and they live in places that have the things they need. (K-ESS3-1)

LS1.C: Organization for Matter and Energy Flow in Organisms Plants need water and light to live and grow. (K-LS1-1)

Objectives Students will be able to:

- Identify plants as living things.
- Explain that plants need water and light to live and grow.
- Explain that living things live in places that have the things that they need.

Science Vocabulary

need

ENGAGE

Tap Prior Knowledge

- Say: **Imagine that I give each of you a plant. What would you do to make sure it stays alive?** (Possible answers: I would water it. I would put it in a sunny place.) Write students' ideas on chart paper and read them aloud.
- Encourage students to discuss why they know that plants are living things. Remind them of the questions they asked themselves in the previous lesson to help identify living things: **Does it grow and change? Is it alive?**

EXPLORE

Preview the Lesson

- Show pages 6–7 and have students take a picture walk, discussing what they observe. Ask: **What types of plants do you see?** (trees, flowers/flowering plant)
- Direct students' attention to the small picture of the trees on page 6. Ask: **What is happening in this picture?** (Trees are growing in a forest. The sun is shining on the trees.) Direct students to look at the large picture of the flowering plant. Ask: **What is happening in this picture?** (It is raining. The rain is falling on the plant.)

Set a Purpose and Read

- Read the lesson's main heading. Tell students to listen to find out about plants and what they need to live.
- Have students listen as you read aloud pages 6–7.

EXPLAIN

Identify What Plants Need

- Direct students to revisit the pictures on pages 6–7. Reread the heading and text aloud. Point to the boldface word *need* on page 6 and say it. Have students point to other places on pages 6–7 where they find the word *need*. Say: **A *need* is something a living thing must have to stay alive.** Ask: **What do you need to live?** (Possible answers: food, water, air, a place to live) Have students contrast needs with things they merely want, such as toys or games.
- Point to the picture of the trees on page 6. Read the caption: **Most plants *need* light. These trees get light from the sun.** Point to the picture of the flowering plant and read the caption on page 7: **Rain can give plants the water that they *need*.** Discuss and review where the bear and plants on page 4 get the things they need.
- Point out to students that living things such as plants live in places that have the things that they need, such as water and light.

Describe Plants As Living Things

- Reread the heading and text on page 6. Point to the picture of the flowering plant. Say: **This plant is alive. It grows and changes. It is a living thing.** Point to the picture of the trees. Say: **The trees are also plants. They grow and change. They are living things.**
- Review that all living things need certain things to stay alive. Point to the picture of the flowering plant. Say: **Like all living things, plants need things to stay alive.** Ask: **Which need is being met in this picture?** (Students should identify the rain as providing the water that the plant needs.) Tell students that water soaks into the ground after it rains. Roots are plant parts that take in this water. Point to the picture of the trees. Ask: **Which need is being met in this**

picture? (Students should identify the sun as providing the light that the trees need.) Tell students that a plant's leaves use light to make food.

- Have students turn to a partner to discuss the following questions: **What might happen if a plant didn't get water or light?** (Possible answers: It would dry up, get limp, or die.) **What might happen if a plant got too little or too much water?** (Possible answers: It might dry up, die, or wash away.)
- Read aloud the caption for the trees on page 6. Say: **Imagine the world with no light. What would it be like?** (It would be dark; there would be no plants.) Ask: **What might happen if these trees did not get enough light?** (They would die.)

ELABORATE

Find Out More About Trees

Step 1: Have students work in small groups to discuss what they know about different types of trees. Invite groups to go outside or look out a window to describe the trees that they see, or have them share about trees that they have seen before. Provide picture books and/or Internet resources about trees for groups to explore. Ask students to find pictures of trees getting either light or water.
Step 2: If time permits, have students draw a picture in their science notebook of the tree they explore, showing the tree as it gets either light or water. Assist students to write words describing their trees and the need that is being met in their pictures.

Extend Your Thinking About Watering Plants

Ask: **Do you think plants need to be watered each day?** Explain to students that many houseplants do not need water daily, but that watering each week often is necessary. Then show students pictures of plants that can survive with little water, such as cactus plants. Discuss with students that these plants live in places where it rarely rains. The plants are able to store water inside them so that they can go for long periods of time without water. Invite students to explore different pictures of cactus plants, recording a drawing of one in their science notebook.

EVALUATE

Have students record their answer to the Wrap It Up question in their science notebook.

Wrap It Up!

1. RECALL **Name two things that plants need to live and grow.** (Possible answers: They need water and light to live.)

SCIENCE MISCONCEPTIONS

Watering Plants Too Much

All plants need water, but too much water is not healthy for a plant. Some of the same symptoms of poor plant health are seen when a plant is given too much water as when it is not given enough. Browning of leaves, spots on leaves, and wilting of leaves are all conditions that can be caused by over-watering or under-watering. For many plants, it is important to let the soil dry out between waterings but not let it stay dry for too long.

READING CONNECTION

Identify the Main Topic

With prompting and support, identify the main topic and retell key details of a text.

Guide students as they identify the main topic and retell key details of this lesson. For example, as you preview the lesson in the EXPLORE section, point out the main heading on page 6. Read it aloud for students. Then ask: **From this heading, what do you think is the main topic of this lesson?** (Students should recognize that the main topic is what plants need.) As you move through the EXPLAIN section, have students use key details from the text and the pictures to explain what plants need.

What Plants Need

NEXT GENERATION SCIENCE STANDARDS | DISCIPLINARY CORE IDEAS
ESS3.A: Natural Resources Living things need water, air, and resources from the land, and they live in places that have the things they need. (K-ESS3-1)

Objectives **Students will be able to:**

- Identify that plants need water, air, and resources from the land.
- Explain that plants live in places that have the things they need to live.

ENGAGE

Tap Prior Knowledge

- Ask students if they have ever planted seeds in a pot or garden at home. Ask: **Where did you plant your seeds?** (Possible answers: in a pot with soil; in the dirt; in the ground) **After your seeds grew into plants, what did you do to keep your plants healthy and alive?** (I watered them; I placed them by a sunny window; I gave them space to grow.)
- Have students share experiences about planting seeds and caring for young plants. Encourage students to include what they provided for the plants to help them live and grow healthy.

EXPLORE

Preview the Lesson

- Show pages 8–9 and have students take a picture walk with you. Have students share what they observe. Ask: **What living things do you see?** (plants) **Where do these plants live?** (in the ground; in the soil)
- Direct students to look closely at the base of the plant's stem in order to see that it is growing out of the soil. Discuss how these plants live in the soil and have roots, which we cannot see, that are growing below the soil. The roots take in water and help hold the plant in place.

Set a Purpose and Read

- Read the lesson's main heading. Tell students to listen to find out about some things plants need to live.
- Have students listen as you read aloud pages 8–9.

EXPLAIN

Identify What Plants Need

- Reread page 8 aloud. Then direct students to look at the picture. Say: **This plant is a living thing. We know that plants need water and light to grow. What else do plants need?** (space and air) Explain to students that air is all around us. We cannot see it, but we breathe it, and plants use it to make food and to live, too.
- Read aloud the caption text on page 8. Point to the soil below the plants in the picture. Say: **Some plants must have soil to grow.** Ask: **Have you ever seen soil? What does it look and feel like?** Encourage students to describe what they have observed about soil. Tell students that a caption can tell what is happening in a picture. This caption tells us that the plants shown live and grow in the soil.

Explain That Plants Live in Places That Have the Things They Need to Live

- Have students look closely at the picture of the plants growing in the soil on pages 8–9. Say: **Look at the way these plants are growing in the soil.** Direct students to notice that each plant is a few inches away from the next, giving them each space to grow. Ask: **Why does a plant need space?** (It needs room to grow and stay healthy.) **What might happen if the plants were put in the soil with no space in between each plant?** (Possible answers: The plants might grow into each other as they get bigger; they might not have enough room to grow; they might die.)
- Ask: **What other needs can you see being met in this picture?** (The plants are getting light; they have space to grow; they are getting air; they are planted in soil.) **Why is this a good place for these plants to live?** (This place has all of the things the plants shown in the picture need to live.)

ELABORATE

Find Out More About Plants and Light

Ask: **What do you think will happen to a plant if does not get enough light?** Use a classroom plant with many large leaves to perform a group investigation. Cut out several one-inch squares of aluminum foil. Allow volunteers to attach the aluminum squares to different leaves with paper clips. The foil should only cover a portion of each leaf. After one week, remove the squares. Students should observe that the area under the leaves has changed color. Guide students to understand that plants need light to live, and if they do not get light they will eventually die.

Extend Your Thinking About Plants and Soil

Discuss with students that many plants grow in soil. Plant roots grow down into the soil and hold the plant in place. Plants also take in nutrients and water from the soil through their roots. Provide students with pictures, illustrated books, and/or Internet resources showing one type of plant that lives and grows without soil (also referred to as "air plants" or Tillandsia). Encourage students to explore where these plants might live, and what they need to grow (air, space, light, water). Have students draw pictures of one of these plants in their science notebook.

EVALUATE

Have students record their answer to the Wrap It Up question in their science notebook.

Wrap It Up!

1. IDENTIFY **Plants need water and light. What else do plants need to live and grow?** (water, light, air, space to grow; Some plants also need soil.)

DIFFERENTIATED INSTRUCTION

Extra Support Have students draw a picture of a plant in the classroom or outside (either visible from a classroom window or on the playground). Direct students to include the soil in which the plant is growing, the space it has to grow, and any other need that can be seen (e.g, getting light from the sun, getting water from rain or a watering can). Remind students that plants need these things in order to live.

Challenge Have students draw a picture of a garden in which several plants are growing. Ask students the following questions as they make their drawings: **Do your plants have enough space to grow? Are they getting air? Are they planted in the soil? Can your garden get enough sunlight?** Encourage students to draw their gardens such that all the plants' needs are being met and the plants can live and grow.

READING CONNECTION

Ask and Answer Questions

With prompting and support, ask and answer questions about key details in a text.

Guide students to ask and answer questions about key details in the text. Model this technique as you begin the EXPLAIN section. Say: **Asking yourself questions can help you find the important information in the text. When I start to read, I turn the main heading into a question. In this lesson, I ask myself, "What do plants need?" Then as I read, I look for answers to this question. The answers are key details in the text. What answers can you find to this question?** (Plants must have space, plants need air, and some plants need soil.)

Animals Are Living Things

NEXT GENERATION SCIENCE STANDARDS | DISCIPLINARY CORE IDEAS

ESS3.A: Natural Resources Living things need water, air, and resources from the land, and they live in places that have the things they need. (K-ESS3-1)

Objectives **Students will be able to:**

- Identify animals as living things.
- Explain that animals need water and air to live and grow.
- Explain that animals live in places that have the things they need.

ENGAGE

Tap Prior Knowledge

- Review with students what they know about living things. Say: **Living things grow and change. Living things are alive. Living things have needs that must be met.**
- Invite students to share about a pet that lives at their home. Ask: **Is your pet a living thing? How do you help your pet stay alive?**
- Students should say that their pet is a living thing. Students may say that they feed their pet, give it water, and give it a place to live.

EXPLORE

Preview the Lesson

- Show pages 10–11 and have students take a picture walk with you. Have students share what they observe. Ask: **What animals do you see?** (jaguar, turtle)
- Direct students' attention to the large picture of the jaguar. Ask: **What is happening in this picture?** (The jaguar is drinking water from the stream.) Direct students to look at the small picture of the turtle on page 11. Ask: **What is happening in this picture?** (The turtle is sticking its head up out of the water.)

Set a Purpose and Read

- Read the lesson's main heading. Tell students to listen to find out about animals and what they need to live.
- Have students follow along as you read aloud pages 10–11.

EXPLAIN

Identify Animals As Living Things

- Reread the lesson heading and text on page 10. Point to the picture of the jaguar and say: **This jaguar is alive. It grows and changes. It is a living thing.** Point to the picture of the turtle on page 11 and say: **This turtle is alive. It grows and changes. It is also a living thing.**
- Review how all living things need certain things to live. Have students look at the picture of the jaguar. Read the caption text aloud. Say: **Like other living things, animals need water and air to stay alive.** Ask: **Which need of the jaguar is being met from the stream?** (It is drinking water; it is getting the need for water met.) **How does the Jaguar get air?** (It breathes in the air all around; it breathes through its mouth and nose.)

Identify Animal Needs

- Have students look at the inset picture of the turtle. Read the caption aloud. Ask: **Why do you think the turtle is sticking its head out of the water?** (It needs air to live; it comes up to take a breath of air.) **Which body parts do you think the turtle uses to breathe air?** (It uses its mouth and nose.) Explain that some turtles live on the land, but also swim in the water. Other turtles live in the water, coming out of the water only to breathe and lay their eggs. Invite students to talk about swimming experiences they have had. Ask students to talk about what they do when they need to take a breath of air. Point out that their coming up for air when they swim is the same as the turtle coming up for air.
- Have students discuss the following question with a partner: **What might happen if the jaguar did not get enough water where it lives?** (It might need to find a new place to live where there is enough water; it might die.) **What might happen if the turtle was not able to get enough air?** (It would die.) **Why do the jaguar and the turtle live in these places?** (These places have the things the jaguar and the turtle need to live. Animals live in places that have the things they need.)

ELABORATE

Find Out More About Turtles

My science notebook **Step 1:** Provide students with illustrated books, pictures, or Internet resources about different types of turtles. Be sure to include examples of land turtles and water or sea turtles in your materials. In small groups, have students choose one type of turtle to explore. Read aloud any related text about the turtle and how it gets air. **Step 2:** If time permits, have students draw a picture of the turtle in their science notebook. Help students write descriptive words to accompany their drawings.

Extend Your Thinking About Breathing Air

My science notebook **Step 1:** Discuss with students how all living things need air, whether they are breathing it through a mouth or nose, or using it to make food as a plant does. Discuss how different animals take in air.

- **Step 2:** If time allows, have students brainstorm a list of animals. Remind students that animals live on land and in water. Record their list in the left column of a two-column chart. In the right column, have students share the ways that they think the animals might get air. Provide reference materials for students to explore. Read aloud materials explaining how aquatic animals "breathe" through gills in contrast with the way land animals breathe air through other body parts.

EVALUATE

My science notebook Have students record their answer to the Wrap It Up question in their science notebook.

Wrap It Up!

1. **DRAW CONCLUSIONS** **What are two things animals need to live?** (Animals grow and change. They need air and water to live. Without these things, they would die. Like other living things, animals live in places that have the things they need.

ELL SUPPORT

Show That Animals Are Living Things

Beginning Point to the jaguar. Ask: **Is the jaguar a living thing?** (Yes.) **What is the jaguar doing?** (It is drinking water.) **Does the jaguar need water to live?** (Yes.) Continue by asking yes/no questions about the needs of the turtle shown on page 11.

Intermediate Provide sentence frames to help students describe the needs of living things: *A turtle breathes. It needs (air) to live. A jaguar drinks. It needs (water) to live.*

Advanced Ask students to draw a picture of an animal, such as a pet, meeting one or more of its needs. Work with students to help them write descriptive words about the animal and what need the picture is showing.

READING CONNECTION

Describe the Relationship

With prompting and support, describe the relationship between illustrations and the text in which they appear (e.g., what person, place, thing, or idea in the text an illustration depicts).

Guide students to describe the relationship between the illustrations and the text in this lesson. For example, in the EXPLAIN section when asking students to describe what animals need to live, have students use the pictures of the jaguar and turtle and the captions that accompany them to explain that these living things need water and air to live. Also, in the EXPLAIN section when asking students how the jaguar and turtle get what they need, have students use the pictures to describe which body parts the animals use to breathe air and drink water in order to live.

What Animals Need

NEXT GENERATION SCIENCE STANDARDS | DISCIPLINARY CORE IDEAS

ESS3.A: Natural Resources Living things need water, air, and resources from the land, and they live in places that have the things they need. (K-ESS3-1)

LS1.C: Organization for Matter and Energy Flow in Organisms All animals need food in order to live and grow. They obtain their food from plants or from other animals (K-LS1-1)

Objectives **Students will be able to:**

- Identify that animals need water, air, and resources from the land, and live in places that have the things they need.
- Explain that animals need food in order to live and grow, and that they obtain their food from plants or from other animals.

Science Vocabulary

shelter

ENGAGE

Tap Prior Knowledge

- Review with students what animals need to live. Say: **We know that living things need water and air to live. That means that animals need these things to live. People need these things, too.** Ask: **What else do people need to live?** Invite students to share their ideas about other things that they need to live, such as food, a safe place to live, and people to take care of them.

EXPLORE

Preview the Lesson

- Have students look at the pictures of the frog and caterpillars on page 12. Ask: **What is happening in these pictures?** (A frog is eating a bug. Two caterpillars are eating a leaf.) Next, direct students to look at the picture of the bobcats on page 13. Ask: **What do you notice in this picture?** (Two bobcats are next to each other in what looks like a cave or a big crack in some rocks.)

Set a Purpose and Read

- Read the lesson's main heading. Tell students to listen to find out about some other things that animals need to live.
- Have students follow along as you read aloud pages 12–13.

EXPLAIN

Define Shelter

- Point to the boldface word *shelter* on page 13 and say it. Have students point to other places on pages 12 and 13 where they find the word *shelter*. Say: **A *shelter* is a safe place.** Ask: **Where do you find shelter?** (Possible answers: at home, in school, inside buildings, under umbrellas)
- Point to the picture of the bobcats on page 13 and read the caption on page 12: **These bobcats use this cave as a shelter.** Discuss how the cave provides shelter for these animals by providing a safe place for them to stay.

Describe What Animals Need to Live

- Reread pages 12–13 aloud. Then say: **We know that animals need water and air to live.** Ask: **What else do all animals need?** (food, space to live) Explain that food and space to live are resources that animals get from the land.
- Have students look closely at the pictures of the frog and the caterpillars on page 12. Say: **Animals need food to live.** Ask: **Which animals eat plants for food?** (the caterpillars) **Which animal eats other animals for food?** (the frog) Share with students that animals that eat plants are called herbivores and animals that eat other animals (or meat) are called carnivores.
- Ask: **Why does the frog live in a place where there are grasshoppers?** (The frog needs to live in a place that has what it needs to live. The frog needs food to eat, and frogs eat other small animals, such as grasshoppers, so it lives where there are grasshoppers.) Repeat this question for the caterpillars/leaves and the bobcats/shelter.
- Ask: **What would happen if the caterpillars could not find leaves to eat?** (They would die.) **What might happen if there were no insects where the frog lives?** (It might need to find a new place to live; it would be hungry; it might die.)

- Return again to the picture of the bobcats. Ask: **What need can you see being met in this picture?** (The bobcats found space to live; they found shelter in the cave.) **What might happen if the bobcats did not find a safe place to live?** (Possible answers: They might be eaten by another animal; they might be too cold or hot without shelter; they might die.)

ELABORATE

Find Out More About Carnivores and Herbivores

My science notebook Organize the class into two groups—the Carnivores and the Herbivores. Draw a two-column chart on chart paper with the headings *Carnivores* and *Herbivores*. Explain that a carnivore is a living thing that eats animals (or meat) and an herbivore is a living thing that eats plants. Provide each group with illustrated books, pictures, or Internet resources showing a variety of animals. Help groups to find animals that fall into their category, writing a list of their animals on the chart paper.

Extend Your Thinking About Shelter

My science notebook Say: **Think about places where animals might find shelter.** Remind students that shelter is a safe place in which an animal can stay or live. Make a list of students' ideas on chart paper. Suggestions may include in trees, in caves, in the ground, under leaves. Ask: **Why might these be safe places to live?** (Animals can hide from other animals; animals can be safe from stormy weather; animals can stay dry and warm.) Read the list of possible shelters to the class. Then have students name animals that they know that live in shelters that they listed.

EVALUATE

My science notebook Have students record their answer to the Wrap It Up question in their science notebook.

Wrap It Up!

1. RESTATE **Animals need water and air. What else do animals need to live and grow?** (Animals need food, space to live; and some animals need shelter to live.)

ELL SUPPORT

Identify What Animals Need

Beginning Have pairs of students prepare five index cards: one card for each animal need. Students should illustrate each need with a drawing, and may write the name of the need if they are able. Pairs can use the cards to help form sentences.

Intermediate Provide sentence frames to help students express their ideas: *Animals need to drink (water) to (live). Animals need to eat (food) to (live). Animals need to breathe (air) to (live). Animals need to find (space/shelter) to (live).*

Advanced Have students explain what a day in the life of an animal might be like, including how they might meet their needs during the day.

READING CONNECTION

Understand Unknown Words

With prompting and support, ask and answer questions about unknown words in a text.

Guide students to ask and answer questions about unknown words in the text. For example, in the EXPLAIN section when helping students to define *shelter*, point out the boldfaced term in the text. Explain that this treatment indicates that the term is an important word. Say: **Let's look at the text where the word *shelter* appears. To help me focus on the meaning of an unknown word, I ask myself a question, such as, "What is a shelter?" Then I look for clues to help me answer this question. What clues can you find to answer this question?** (Animals need space. A shelter is a safe place.)

NATIONAL GEOGRAPHIC LEARNING | Think Like a Scientist

Observe

NEXT GENERATION SCIENCE STANDARDS | PERFORMANCE EXPECTATION

K-LS1-1. Use observations to describe patterns of what plants and animals (including humans) need to survive. [Clarification Statement: Examples of patterns could include that animals need to take in food but plants do not; the different kinds of food needed by different types of animals; the requirement of plants to have light; and, that all living things need water.]

Objective **Students will be able to:**

- Use observations to describe patterns of what plants and animals need to survive.

CLASSROOM MANAGEMENT

Time 20 minutes

Teaching Tips Organize the class into groups of 4. Each group should study the pictures on pages 14–15. Encourage groups to discuss what they notice about the needs being met by the plants and animals shown. Remind students of the needs of all living things—water, air, food, and space to live. Also remind students that some plants might need soil to live and some animals might need shelter to live.

What to Expect Students will observe that plants and animals need almost all the same things in order to live. Students should observe that animals take in food, and plants do not (plants make food for themselves through photosynthesis); some animals eat plants while some animals eat other animals; plants need light (to make food) to live; and all living things need water and air to live.

ENGAGE

Tap Prior Knowledge

- Flip through the different lessons that students have completed about what plants and animals need to live. As you turn the pages, remind them about the flowering plants getting water from the rain, the trees getting light from the sun, the small green plants growing in the soil, the jaguar drinking water from the stream, the turtle coming up for air, the frog eating the grasshopper, the caterpillars eating the leaf, and the bobcats finding shelter in the cave. Discuss how these all show needs of plants and animals being met. Ask: **What do all animals need?** (All animals need water, air, food, and space to live. Some animals also need shelter.) **What do all plants need?** (Plants need water, air, light, and space to grow. Some plants also need soil.)

Preview the Lesson

- Tell students to listen as you read aloud the lesson's main heading. Explain that when you observe something, you look very closely at it. You pay attention to what something looks like. You notice what something is doing. Then tell students that in this lesson, they will work with a small group to observe, or look for what plants and animals need to live, and describe these needs. Tell them to look for patterns in how the needs of plants and animals are the same and different. Finally, you might ask students to observe things humans need and describe those needs.

Set a Purpose and Read

- Have students follow along as you read aloud pages 14–15.

EXPLORE

Describe What Plants and Animals Need to Live

- Place students in their groups of four. Say: **We've learned that all living things have certain needs and that a need is something that a living thing must have to live. Now it is your turn. Examine each photo. Discuss the photos in your group. As a group, decide what need is being met for the living thing in each photo.**
- Allow student groups to observe each picture. As necessary, identify the different plants and

animals shown. If a group is struggling, use the following ideas to prompt discussion:

- Point to the picture of the bird on page 14. Ask: **What is this fieldfare bird doing?** (eating) **What need is this bird meeting?** (need for food) Allow students to discuss their answers among themselves. If they are still struggling, continue questioning using the photos on page 15 as a focal point.
- As you point to the panda, ask: **What is the panda doing?** (The panda is eating leaves/ plants.) **What need is the panda meeting?** (The panda is meeting its need for food.)
- Point to the picture of the zebras and ask: **What are the zebras doing?** (drinking water) **Why do you think the zebras are doing this?** (The zebras need water to live. They are drinking water to meet this need.)
- Point to the picture of the daffodils and ask: **What is happening in this picture?** (It is raining.) **How is the rain helping the daffodils to get what they need?** (Rain is water. The daffodils need water to live. The rain is providing water for the plants.)
	- Say: Humans are living things. Ask: **What needs do you have?** (Accept any reasonable response.) Ask: **How do you meet your needs to survive?** (We eat food, drink water, breathe air, and live in houses or apartments.)
- Use these additional questions to assist struggling groups:
	- Point to the picture of the lettuce plants and ask: **Describe how the lettuce is planted.** (Students should note that the lettuce is planted in rows with spaces in between each row, and that the lettuce is planted in the soil.) Ask: **How is the lettuce getting what it needs here?** (The lettuce has space to grow. The sun is giving the lettuce the light it needs to live.)
	- Ask: **What other need is being met by all of the living things in these pictures?** (the need for air) **How are the living things meeting this need?** (They are taking in some of the air that surrounds them.)

SCIENCE AND ENGINEERING PRACTICES

Analyzing and Interpreting Data

- In this activity, students use observations to describe patterns in order to answer scientific questions about how animals survive. Ask: **What is similar about what plants and animals need to survive?** (Possible answer: They both need food, water, air, and space.) **What is different about what they need?** (Possible answer: Animals need to take in food; plants do not. Accept all answers supported by evidence.)

Connections to Nature of Science
Scientific Knowledge is Based on Empirical Evidence

- Discuss with students how scientists look for patterns and order when making observations about the world. Point out that when they make observations about patterns, they are thinking like scientists.

CROSSCUTTING CONCEPTS

Patterns

- Say: **Scientists look for patterns and order when making observations about the world. Patterns in the natural and human designed world can be observed and used as evidence. Encourage students to link the concept of patterns to other disciplines of science.** Ask: **Can you think of something that is a pattern in earth science or physical science?** (Possible answers: day and night, seasons)

Observe (continued)

EXPLORE (continued)

Identify Similar Needs

- After students have identified the need being met by the living things in each photo, have students work in their groups to identify the pictures that show similar needs being met. Circulate among groups. Use the questions below to help groups that are struggling to group the images.
    - Say: **Point to two pictures that show an animal getting what it needs for food.** (Student should point to the pictures of the bird and the panda.) Ask the group: **Which animal eats plants for food?** (panda) **Which animal eats other animals for food?** (fieldfare bird)
    - Have another volunteer point to pictures that show a living thing meeting the need for water. (The student should point to the zebras and the daffodils.) Ask the group: **From where are these living things getting water?** (The zebras are drinking water from a watering hole. The daffodils are getting water from the rain.)
    - Point to the picture of the lettuce plants. Say: **This picture shows lettuce plants living in soil with space to grow and light from the sun.** Ask: **Which other picture shows a plant getting light from the sun, which it needs to live?** (the picture of the daffodil)

EXPLAIN

Share How Living Things Are Meeting Their Needs and Identify Patterns

- After groups have completed their discussions, have a representative from each group share one of their findings. For example, five different students could identify the needs being met in each picture. (bird–food, panda–food; daffodils–water; zebras–water, lettuce–space and soil and light) Then other representatives could identify the pictures that show the same need. (bird and panda–food; daffodils and zebras–water; daffodils and lettuce–light; all photos–air) Finally, have students describe the patterns they have observed. For example, students could point out that animals eat food, but plants do not. Others could explain that animals drink to get water and plants get water from water that falls from the sky and soaks into the soil.
- Say: **Scientists know that they need to use observations to describe patterns in the natural world in order to answer scientific questions.** Ask: **In what ways did you think like a scientist as you completed this activity?** (I made observations and looked for patterns, just as a scientist does.)

ELABORATE

Extend Your Thinking About How Plants Get What They Need

My science notebook

Help students find out more about how plants get the food, water, and air they need to live. Draw on chart paper a diagram of a simple plant, showing and labeling its parts—leaves, stem, roots. Organize students into three groups, and assign each group one of the three main plant parts. Provide illustrated books, plant diagrams, or Internet resources showing plants parts and their functions. Work with each group, exploring and reading text about their plant part and how this part helps a plant meet its needs. Groups should find that green plants use light, water, and air to make food in their leaves; that stems hold up the leaves (and sometimes make food), and that water and food move through the stem; and that roots take in water (and other nutrients), which moves up to the leaves. After groups share their findings, have students draw a diagram in their science notebook showing the parts of a plant.

EVALUATE

My science notebook

Ask students these questions. Have them record their answers in their science notebook.

1. **RECALL What do living things need to survive?** (water, air, food, space to live; Plants also need light to live. Some plants need soil. Some animals need shelter.)
2. **IDENTIFY Which pictures show living things getting the air they need to live? Explain.** (Every picture shows living things getting the air they need to live. We cannot see air, but I know that the animals are breathing the air and the plants are getting the air they need to live.)
3. **APPLY Why do you think there are no pictures showing plants eating food?** (Plants do not eat food. They make their own food in their leaves.)

RUBRICS

Teacher Rubric Use the scale descriptions to guide your assessment of the student's work. Assess each item separately, and then decide on one overall score, using the following scale:

4: Student performs with thorough understanding.
3: Student performs with adequate understanding.
2: Student performs with basic understanding.
1: Student performs with limited understanding.

Rubric	Scale			
The student worked with a group to closely observe pictures showing the needs of plants and animals and identify important details.	4	3	2	1
The student discussed observations with others in a group.	4	3	2	1
The student worked with a group to draw conclusions about the needs depicted in the pictures and grouped pictures that showed the same need.	4	3	2	1
The student shared his or her conclusions with others in the class.	4	3	2	1
Overall Score	4	3	2	1

Student Rubric Have students complete a self-evaluation similar to that shown below.

Rubric	Yes	Not Yet
1 I can make careful observations and identify important details and discuss my observations with others in my group.		
2 I can work with a group to draw conclusions about what plants and animals need.		
3 I can work with a group to identify pictures that show the same need being met.		
4 I can explain my group's observations, conclusions, and groupings to others in my class.		

Where Living Things Live

NEXT GENERATION SCIENCE STANDARDS | DISCIPLINARY CORE IDEAS

ESS 3.A: Natural Resources Living things need water, air, and resources from the land, and they live in places that have the things they need. (K-ESS3-1)

Objective Students will be able to:

- Explain that living things live in places that have the things they need.

ENGAGE

Tap Prior Knowledge

- Make a two-column chart on chart paper. Write the following heads, one at the top of each column: *Our Homes*, *Animal and Plant Homes*. Ask students to name different places where people live. Record these ideas under *Our Homes*. (Possible answers: house, apartment, townhouse, manufactured housing)
- Say: **Animals and plants live in different places, too. Where can animals and plants live?** (Possible answers: forest, ocean, park, pond, desert, arctic) Record these ideas under *Animal and Plant Homes*. Discuss ways that plants and animals are able, or have adapted, to live in the wild.

EXPLORE

Preview the Lesson

- Show pages 16–17 and have students share what plants and animals they observe.
- Point to the picture of the nest on page 16. Ask: **What is this a picture of?** (a nest in a tree) Guide students to look at the squirrel in the tree. Ask: **What do you notice about the squirrel in the tree?** (It is sitting on a branch; it is eating something.) Encourage students to share other details that they notice about this forest habitat scene.

Set a Purpose and Read

- Read the lesson's main heading. Tell students to listen to find out about where living things live and how they get what they need there.
- Have students follow along as you read aloud pages 16–17.

EXPLAIN

Discuss Where Living Things Live

- Direct students to look at the background picture of the habitat. Say: **This picture shows a place where plants and animals live.** Ask: **What plants and animals do you see in the picture?** (trees and a squirrel) Have students describe the habitat that the trees and the squirrel live in. Explain that this habitat is called a forest.
- Ask: **What other plants and animals might live in a forest?** (Possible answers: lots of trees, small plants, insects, deer, rabbits, birds) Say: **Many different plants and animals live in a forest. There is sunlight, soil, rain, and air for plants. There are places for animals to live that are close to the ground or high up in the trees.**
- Say: **Plants and animals can live in many places all over the world. They live in places that have the things that meet their needs.** Ask: **Why do fish live in the ocean?** (Possible answers: Fish live in the ocean because they need to be in water to live, because their food and homes are in the ocean, because they use gills to breathe, and because they would die if they came onto the land.) **Why might the desert be a good home for a cactus plant (or a plant that does not need a lot of water to live)?** (Possible answers: Cactus plants do not need a lot of water to live. The desert is very dry. It does not rain a lot there.)

Explain How Living Things Get What They Need From Where They Live

- Direct students to again look at the picture of the squirrel on page 17. Say: **The squirrel gets what it needs from the forest.** Ask: **What does the squirrel need to live?** (air, water, food, shelter) Point to the picture of the nest on page 16. Ask: **What does the squirrel use its nest for?** (to live in; as a home; for shelter) **Why might the squirrel build its nest up high in a tall tree?** (Possible answers: to keep itself dry and warm, away from the wet ground; to stay away from danger; to protect itself from animals that live on the ground that might eat it)

- Direct students to look at what the squirrel is doing with its front paws. Read the caption aloud: **What need is this squirrel meeting?** (The squirrel is eating, meeting its need for food.) **Why is the forest a good home for the squirrel?** (Possible answer: There are trees for squirrels to live and stay safe in.)
- Point to the picture of the tree on pages 16–17. Say: **Plants need air, light, water, and space to grow.** Ask: **What needs of this tree are met in the forest?** (Possible answer: The need for light from the sun, air, and space to live and grow.) **How do you think the tree gets the water that it needs?** (from the rain)

ELABORATE

Find Out More About a Forest Habitat

Help students work in small groups to explore a forest habitat. Explain that a habitat is a place where plants and animals live. Encourage groups to choose one forest plant and one forest animal to research. Provide illustrated books, pictures of forests, or Internet resources for groups to use to identify their living things. Assist students with reading text and captions as necessary. Have students draw pictures of their plant and animal in their science notebook. Help students to record how each living thing meets its needs living in the forest.

Extend Your Thinking About Animal Nests

Say: **Birds make nests for shelter and to protect their young.** Ask: **What other animals make nests?** Students learned that squirrels make nests in trees. Encourage students to share other nest-making animals that they may know. Discuss how egg-laying animals, such as wasps, and snakes, use nests to protect their eggs and young from weather and predators.

EVALUATE

Have students record their answer to the Wrap It Up question in their science notebook.

Wrap It Up!

1. IDENTIFY **What are the needs a tree and a squirrel can meet in a forest?** (They both can get water, space to live, and air. The tree can get sunlight and make its food. It can grow in soil. The squirrel can get shelter and food.)

TEACHING WITH TECHNOLOGY

Identify Needs Being Met

Project the lesson on a whiteboard. Have one student point to the animal on the branch. Ask: **What type of animal is this?** (squirrel) Say: **Circle something that the squirrel uses in the forest to meet a need.** (The student could circle the acorn in its paws, the nest in the tree, or the tree itself.) Ask: **What need is the [acorn, nest, tree] meeting for the squirrel?** Have a second student circle something different that meets another one of the squirrel's needs. Continue until the acorn, the nest and/or the tree are circled.

READING CONNECTION

Describe the Relationship

With prompting and support, describe the relationship between illustrations and the text in which they appear (e.g., what person, place, thing, or idea in the text an illustration depicts).

Guide students as they describe the relationship between illustrations and text in this lesson. For example, in the EXPLAIN section when students are describing where plants and animals live, have students use the pictures of the forest scene along with the text explaining the environment to describe plant and animal habitats. Also in the EXPLAIN section when students are explaining how living things get what they need from where they live, direct them to use the picture of the squirrel and the tree in the forest along with the text to describe how these living things get what they need in the forest.

Make a Model

NEXT GENERATION SCIENCE STANDARDS | PERFORMANCE EXPECTATION

K-ESS3-1. Use a model to represent the relationship between the needs of different plants or animals (including humans) and the places they live. [Clarification Statement: Examples of relationships could include that deer eat buds and leaves, therefore, they usually live in forested areas; and, grasses need sunlight so they often grow in meadows. Plants, animals, and their surroundings make up a system.]

Objective Students will be able to:

- Use a model to represent the relationship between the needs of different plants or animals and the place they live.

CLASSROOM MANAGEMENT

Suggested Materials writing and drawing materials such as pencils, colored pencils, crayons, or markers

Time 10 minutes for group review; 10 minutes for planning and partner discussions; 15 minutes for making models; 10 minutes for sharing models

Teaching Tips As a class, review the picture of the meadow habitat on pages 18–19. Have students discuss with a partner the needs that they see being met. Then have students work independently to draw their picture. Remind students that living things need air, water, food, and shelter/space to live. Plants also need light, and some plants need soil. Explain that deer eat leaves and buds from trees and grasses for food.

What to Expect Students will observe that the deer, the trees, and the grasses all survive in the meadow because they get what they need there. The deer eats the leaves and buds from the plants, and the grasses get plenty of sunlight out in the open meadow. The trees have trunks that lift their leaves to catch the sunlight. The deer can find shelter in the trees, and the grasses and trees have space to grow. Students will also note that both the plants and animals get the air they need. Students may not note how the plants and animals get the water they need. Explain that rain provides water for the plants, and that deer find puddles, ponds, and/or streams nearby to get their water.

ENGAGE

Set the scene.

- Talk with students about the plants and animals that they have seen in person and in the previous lessons of this text. Ask: **What do you know about what all living things need to live?** (Students may say that all living things need air, water, food, and shelter/space to grow. They may also say that living things get what they need from where they live.) Remind students that plants also need light to live, and many need soil as well. Also note that some animals just need space to live while others need some form of shelter.

Observe and plan.

- Read the introductory text on page 18 aloud. Say: **Look at the picture of the meadow scene. Many plants and animals live in a meadow. The meadow provides the things they need to live.** Say: **You will make a model to show living things meeting their needs in a meadow.** Explain that in this case, the model students make will be a drawing showing the living things in the meadow and how those living things meet their needs in the meadow.

- Guide students as they plan their models. Have partners discuss the needs of plants and animals they observe are being met in the meadow scene on pages 18–19. Ask:
    - **What plants and animals do you see in the meadow?**
    - **What needs are the plants meeting?**
    - **What needs are the animals meeting?**
    - **What other living things may be in the meadow or the trees surrounding the meadow?**
- Have students share with their partner what they plan to draw in their models.

  Example: I looked at the picture and saw a deer, lots of grass with flowers, and trees in the background. I plan to draw a model of a meadow showing how these plants and animals get what they need.

EXPLORE

Draw your model.

My science notebook Have students draw a picture of a deer living in a meadow. Remind students to include the different plants they observed.

- Ask students questions to help them produce complete drawings:
    - **Where are the plants?**
    - **Where are the animals?**
    - **What is shining light on the plants?**
    - **What can the deer eat for food?**
    - **Where might the deer find shelter?**
    - **What surrounds all the plants and animals you see?**
- Have students draw their models in their science notebook.

SCIENCE AND ENGINEERING PRACTICES

Developing and Using Models

- In this activity, students made a model of a meadow to represent how different plants and animals meet their needs in a meadow. Discuss with students other models they could make that would represent relationships among animals and plants. (Students may suggest making a model of a different place in nature and the animals and plants that live there.)

CROSSCUTTING CONCEPTS

Systems and System Models

- Discuss with students that their model of a meadow is a system, and a system in the natural world has parts that work together. Encourage students to link the concept of a system to other science lessons they have had. For example, all the different parts of weather make up a system.

Make a Model (continued)

EXPLAIN

Share and explain your model.

- Have students share their completed model with a partner. Help students explain what they drew, prompting partners to ask:
  - **How does the deer meet its needs for food in the meadow?**
  - **How do the plants meet their need for light in the meadow?**
  - **What other needs did you show and label in your model?**
- Help students draw conclusions about why these plants and animals live in a meadow. Ask: **Why is a meadow a good home for deer and grasses? (**Example explanation: My model of a meadow has a deer eating grasses and flowers, trees all around the outside of the meadow, and the sun shining over the meadow. The deer is getting food by eating the grass and flowers, and it is breathing the air that is all around it. The deer can also hide from another animal in the tall grass or behind a group of trees. The grass, flowers, and trees get a lot of sunlight out in the open meadow. They also get the air they need and have lots of space to grow. The meadow is a good home for the deer, the grasses, flowers, and trees because they all can get what they need there.)

Make changes.

- After sharing and explaining their models with a partner, ask: **What changes could you make to your model to show more needs being met in the meadow? (**Students' answers will vary. Possible answer: I showed the deer eating grass. I could change my model to show a second deer hiding from another animal in the grass. I drew the sun shining on the plants. I could change my model to show rain falling on part of the meadow so the plants get watered.)
- Say: **Scientists often use models to represent the way the natural world works.** Ask: **In what ways did you think like a scientist as you completed this activity?** (I made a model of a meadow and made observations and looked for patterns, just as a scientist does.)
- Ask: **In what ways do you have your needs met in order to live and grow?** (I eat food, drink water, live in a home, and breathe air.) Ask: **Where do people get things they need?** (People get their needs met from the place we live in, planet Earth. Everything we use comes from a natural resource.) Ask: **Why do we get everything we need from natural resources?** (Things in the natural world work together to meet the needs for living things so plants, animals, and people can all survive.)

ELABORATE

Find Out More About Meadows

- **Step 1:** Help students to find out more about what types of plants and animals live successfully in a meadow environment. Provide illustrated books, pictures, or Internet resources showing living things in meadows. Read text and discuss findings with students.
  Step 2: Have students draw pictures of the different plants and animals that they discover also live in meadows. Encourage students to label the needs that these plants and animals can meet by living there.

Humans Meet Their Needs

- Point out to students that humans are living things. Discuss with students how humans meet their needs in the places where they live.

EVALUATE

My science notebook Check to make sure students have recorded their models in their science notebook. Then ask students these questions. Have them record the answers in their science notebook.

1. **IDENTIFY What living things can you find in a meadow?** (plants and animals, such as deer, grass, flowers, trees)
2. **DRAW CONCLUSIONS Why is a meadow a good place for deer and grass to live?** (Deer can eat grass, find shelter in tall grasses and trees, and get air from all around. Grasses can get plenty of sunlight, have lots of space to grow, and get air from all around. Rain gives the grasses water.)

RUBRICS

Teacher Rubric Use the scale descriptions to guide your assessment of the student's work. Assess each item separately, and then decide on one overall score, using the following scale:

4: Student performs with thorough understanding.
3: Student performs with adequate understanding.
2: Student performs with basic understanding.
1: Student performs with limited understanding.

Rubric	Scale			
The student closely observed a meadow environment and discussed observations in detail.	4	3	2	1
The student planned and made a model that served as a basis for explaining how living things survive in a meadow environment.	4	3	2	1
The student shared the model with others, explaining details of the model, labels used, and needs being met.	4	3	2	1
The student revisited the model, critiquing its representation, and proposing possible revisions based on their own review and feedback from others.	4	3	2	1
Overall Score	4	3	2	1

Student Rubric Have students complete a self-evaluation similar to that shown below.

Rubric	Yes	Not Yet
1 I can make observations and plan for making a model of a meadow.		
2 I can organize my ideas, draw, and label a detailed meadow model.		
3 I can explain my meadow model to others		
4 I can revise my model based on what others say and my own conclusions to make it better.		

Living Things Change the Places They Live

NEXT GENERATION SCIENCE STANDARDS | DISCIPLINARY CORE IDEAS
ESS2.E: Biogeology Plants and animals can change their environment. (K-ESS2-2)

Objective **Students will be able to:**
- Identify how plants and animals can change their environment.

ENGAGE

Tap Prior Knowledge

- Ask: **Have you ever seen a tree growing near a sidewalk? What did you notice about the sidewalk?** Students who have seen this may say that part of the tree was growing under the sidewalk or through the sidewalk. They may note that the sidewalk was cracked, broken, or popping up. Discuss what students think might have caused the sidewalk to break.

EXPLORE

Preview the Lesson

- Show pages 20–21 and have students share what they observe. Ask: **What living things do you see?** (tree, prairie dog)
- Direct students' attention to the large picture of the prairie dog. Ask: **What is happening in this picture?** (The prairie dog is looking out from a hole in the ground.) Direct students to look at the small picture of the tree on page 20. Ask: **What is happening in this picture?** (The tree is growing on top of a big rock.)

Set a Purpose and Read

- Read the lesson's main heading. Tell students to listen as you read aloud the text to find out about how living things change the places where they live.
- Have students follow along as you read aloud pages 20–21.

EXPLAIN

Describe How Plants Can Change Where They Live

- Point to the small picture of the tree and read the caption. Say: **Living things can change the place where they live. This tree is growing on a big rock. Look closely at the tree's roots. Describe the roots.** (Students may say that the roots are very big and long. They are growing all over the rock.) Say: **Describe the rock.** (Students may say that it is big and flat with cracks in it.)
- Ask: **What are the tree's roots doing to the rock?** (They are growing in the cracks; they are making bigger cracks in the rock.) **What might happen as the roots grow bigger?** (The roots might make the cracks bigger and break the rock into pieces.)
- Ask: **How can trees change where they live?** (Their roots can grow into rocks and break the rocks apart.) **Where else might you see a tree's roots growing and changing things around it?** (in a sidewalk; coming up through the ground; pushing into another tree or nonliving thing such as rocks or human-made objects placed in the path of a tree's root system)

Describe How Animals Can Change Where They Live

- Reread the text on page 21. Point to the picture of the prairie dog and read the caption. Say: **Animals can change things about where they live. This prairie dog dug the hole it is in.** Ask: **Why did the prairie dog dig a hole in the ground?** (to make a shelter for itself; to live in)
- Invite students to describe the ground around the hole verses the ground where the hole was dug. Ask: **What do you think the ground was like before the prairie dog made its hole?** (It was flat and smooth like the rest of the ground around the hole is now.) **How has the prairie dog changed the way the ground looks?** (It dug a hole into the ground; the ground is not flat and smooth in that spot anymore.)

- Ask students to infer how other animals might change where they live. Ask questions to help facilitate ideas and discussion, such as: **How might a dog change a yard? How might a woodpecker change a tree? How might a beaver change a river? How might a worm change the soil? How might ants change the sand?** Encourage students to help you generate a list of different animals and discuss how these animals may change where they live by digging, pecking, building a dam, moving soil or sand, or other types of physical changes.

ELABORATE

Find Out More About Prairie Dogs

My science notebook

Step 1: Help students working in small groups to research prairie dogs. Provide illustrated books and Internet resources for students to explore. Have students try to find pictures of prairie dogs' underground homes, explaining that these homes are called *burrows*. Discuss how these animals change where they live by digging many holes and making piles of dirt where they dig.
Step 2: Have students find and draw a picture in their science notebook of prairie dogs in burrows.

Extend Your Thinking About Digging and the Environment

My science notebook

Step 1: Say: **A prairie dog can change the ground where it lives by digging holes for shelter.** Ask: **What other living things dig holes, changing where they live?** Lead the class in a brainstorming session about how different living things dig in the ground, changing it. Remind students that people are also living things, and that we dig for many different reasons, changing the land around us.
Step 2: If time permits, invite students to choose one living thing from the list, draw a picture, and write words in their science notebook (with assistance if necessary) showing how this "digger" is changing where it lives.

EVALUATE

My science notebook

Have students record the answer to the Wrap It Up question in their science notebook.

Wrap It Up!

1. EXPLAIN **How does the prairie dog change the ground where it lives?** (It digs a hole into the ground.)

SCIENCE BACKGROUND

Living in Burrows

Prairie dogs dig and live in underground tunnel systems called burrows. Their burrows can be very extensive, including many different pockets of space designated for different living situations, such as sleeping, baby care, and even toilets. When prairie dogs dig their holes, they mark their entrances with mounds of packed dirt. Prairie dogs keep watch for any predators by waiting and listening in chambers near these exits. Much time is spent digging, building, and rebuilding these burrow systems. Other animals such as snakes and burrowing owls also benefit from these burrows, sharing these homes with the prairie dogs.

READING CONNECTION

Describe the Connection

With prompting and support, describe the connection between two individuals, events, ideas, or pieces of information in a text.

Guide students to describe the connection between two pieces of information in the text. For example, in the EXPLAIN section when students describe how a tree can change where it lives, have students note the connection between the roots of the tree growing in the rock and the rock breaking into pieces. Also in the EXPLAIN section when students describe how a prairie dog changes where it lives, have students explain how prairie dogs digging holes in the ground change the land where they live.

Explain Change

NEXT GENERATION SCIENCE STANDARDS | PERFORMANCE EXPECTATION

K-ESS2-2. Construct an argument supported by evidence for how plants and animals (including humans) can change the environment to meet their needs. [Clarification Statement: Examples of plants and animals changing their environment could include a squirrel digs in the ground to hide its food and tree roots can break concrete.]

NEXT GENERATION SCIENCE STANDARDS | DISCIPLINARY CORE IDEA

ESS3.C: Human Impacts on Earth Systems Things that people do to live comfortably can affect the world around them. But they can make choices that reduce their impacts on the land, water, air, and other living things. (secondary to K-ESS2-2)

Objective Students will be able to:

- Construct an argument supported by evidence for how plants and animals (including humans) can change the environment to meet their needs.

CLASSROOM MANAGEMENT

Time 20 minutes

Teaching Tips Pair students. Each pair should study the pictures on pages 22–23. Encourage pairs to discuss what they notice about the environment in each picture. Remind students of the needs of all living things—water, air, food, space to live and grow, shelter. Also remind them that plants need light and some need soil.

What to Expect Students will observe that both plants and animals can change where they live and do so in order to meet their needs. Students should observe animals (beaver, skunk, woodpecker, humans) changing where they live by building homes and digging holes. Students should observe a tree's roots changing where the tree lives by cracking the sidewalk. Students should conclude that these plants and animals change the land in an effort to get what they need (food, shelter, space to live and grow, and materials they need).

ENGAGE

Tap Prior Knowledge

- Review with students the different lessons that they have completed about where plants and animals live, how they meet their needs where they live, and how they can change where they live. Flip through pages 16–21.

Point out different ways that the living things shown changed the places where they live. For example, the squirrel changed the tree by using twigs and other materials to build a next in the tree; the tree roots cracked the rock; and the prairie dog dug holes in the ground. Discuss how these living things all find what they need where they live and sometimes change where they live in the process. Remind them that people also change the land as they build things, grow food, make roads, or dig holes to get the materials they need.

EXPLORE

Preview the Lesson

- As a class, look at the different pictures of the plants and animals on pages 22–23. Ask: **What is happening in each picture? How are living things changing where they live?** (Students may say that the animals and people are building homes or shelters, digging in the dirt, or pecking holes in trees, using resources to meet their needs, and that the tree is moving the sidewalk.)

Set a Purpose and Read

- Tell students to listen as you read aloud the main heading and text on page 22. Explain that for this lesson, students will work with a partner to observe living things changing where they live in some way and describe the change. Students will then work together to explain how these changes help living things meet a specific need.
- Have students follow along as you read aloud pages 22–23.

Describe How Plants and Animals Change Where They Live

- Have each student sit with a partner. Say: **Work with your partner. Look at the change happening in each picture. The living things shown are making these changes. You need to work together to look closely at each picture to discover how the change is being made and explain why.**
- Allow pairs to observe and discuss the change shown in each picture. As necessary, identify the different organisms shown and read the captions. If a pair is struggling, use the following ideas to prompt discussion:
  - Guide students to look at the picture of the beaver. Ask: **What is the beaver doing?** (It is chewing on a piece of wood; it is cutting a piece of wood into pieces with its teeth.) **Where might the beaver have gotten this wood?** (It may have cut down a tree with its teeth; it may have found it in the forest.)
  - Guide students to look at the four smaller pictures on page 23. Ask: **How are living things changing the places where they live here?** Invite students to discuss one picture at a time.
  - Point to the picture of the skunk and read the question aloud: **How does the skunk change the land?** (It digs a hole in the ground.)
  - Point to the picture of the tree and read the question aloud: **How does the tree change the sidewalk?** (Its roots grow under the sidewalk and push it up off the ground; it breaks up the sidewalk.)
  - Point to the picture of the woodpecker and read the question aloud: **How does the woodpecker change the tree?** (It is pecking through the wood; it is making holes in the tree trunk.)
  - Point to the picture of the earth-moving machine and read the question aloud: **How do people change the land?** (There is a person running the machine to dig in the ground; the machine is lifting up buckets full of dirt and rocks from the ground, making a hole.)

Show How the Change Helps Meet a Need

- Have pairs look again at the pictures on pages 22–23 of the living things changing the places where they live. Say: **Look at the change in each picture. Think about *why* the living things are making these changes.**
- Again allow pairs to observe and discuss why the living thing is making the change shown in each picture. If a pair is struggling, use the following ideas to prompt discussion:
  - Point to the picture of the beaver. Ask: **Why do you think the beaver is cutting wood with its teeth?** (to make smaller pieces of wood to use to build a home) Ask: **What need would a home like this meet?** (the need for shelter)
- Continue providing support to struggling pairs by asking questions such as the following:
  - Point to the picture of the skunk. Ask: **Why might the skunk dig in the ground?** (to find something; to get food to make a

SCIENCE AND ENGINEERING PRACTICES

Engaging in Argument from Evidence

- In this activity, students construct an argument about how the animals and plants in the photos change the environment to meet their needs. Discuss with students some of the ways people change their environments to meet their own needs. (Possible answers: People plant trees to make shade in our yards, they plant vegetable gardens to grow food to eat.)

CROSSCUTTING CONCEPTS

Systems and System Models

- Say: **A system is something that has different parts that work together to make a whole.** Ask: **How do you think small parts such as a beaver's teeth fit into a system?** (The teeth help a beaver cut down trees. The beaver makes a dam and home for itself. The dam makes a pond and makes homes for other animals.)

Explain Change (continued)

EXPLORE (continued)

shelter) Explain that skunks often dig for food such as insect grubs, which live in the soil.

- Point to the picture of the tree. Ask: **Why did the tree's roots grow this way?** (The roots need space to grow.)
- Point to the picture of the woodpecker. Ask: **Why does the woodpecker make holes in the tree?** (to get food from inside the tree) Explain that woodpeckers use their sharp beaks to peck away at the wood and their long, sticky tongues to get the food out of the hole.
- Point to the picture of the construction site. Ask: **Why might people be digging up this land?** (Possible answers: to build a home or building; to build a road; to dig for something they need that is in the ground; to make space) Ask: **What do you think people can do to make fewer changes to land, but still meet their needs?** (Possible answers: walk to school instead of driving, give old toys and clothes to somebody else instead of throwing them away, use a glass cup for water instead of buying a bottle of water, recycle aluminum cans)

EXPLAIN

Share How Living Things Are Meeting Their Needs

- After partners have completed their discussions, ask: **What needs are being met by all these changes?** Have a representative from each pair share one of their findings. For example, five different students could identify the changes being made in each picture. (beaver—cutting wood; skunk—digging a hole; tree—breaking the sidewalk; woodpecker—drilling a hole in a tree; machine—digging a hole and removing rocks from the ground) Then other representatives could explain why each change helps a living thing meet a need. (skunk—food or shelter; woodpecker—food; tree—space to grow; beaver—shelter or food; people—materials for building or space to live)
- Allow pairs to reassess their conclusions, and revise them as necessary, based on class discussion.
- Say: **Scientists construct, or make, an argument with evidence to support a claim.** Ask: **In what ways did you think like a scientist as you completed this activity?** (I made observations to explain what might be happening, just as a scientist does.)

ELABORATE

Share More About Why These Plants and Animals Change the Places Where They live.

- If time permits, share additional information about each living thing shown on pages 22–23 and how the changes they make help meet a need.
  - Beavers use the sticks they cut not only to build their homes, but to also build a dam. The dam slows the flow of water in the river where it is built. The beaver then builds a home in the pond that forms behind the dam. Point out that the dam also helps beavers to find food and stay safe.
  - Skunks often dig for food such as insect grubs, which live in the soil. Some skunks also use their long claws to dig a den (a shelter). Skunks also use hollow logs, woodpiles, and people's decks for shelter!
  - A tree's roots need space to grow outward in all directions in order to get the water and nutrients the tree needs and to keep the tree upright. If something is in the way of the root's growth, a root will simply grow through it, or break through it to continue growing.
  - Woodpeckers hammer holes into living and dead trees to find insects and their grubs.
  - Ask students how people might use the materials being dug out of the ground in the photo. Discuss that people use these rocks to help them meet their needs for building materials, gravel for roads and concrete, and countertops, among other things.

Find Out More About Meeting Needs

My science notebook

Step 1: Have students brainstorm other living things that they think might change where they live to meet a need. Record students' ideas on chart paper. Organize students into four groups, and assign each group to one living thing from the list. Provide students with resources; have them research how their living thing meets its need and if it changes the land as it does so. Have students draw a picture in their science notebook of the living thing changing its environment while meeting a need.

Step 2: If time permits, invite groups to share their findings with the class.

EVALUATE

My science notebook

Ask students these questions. Have them record the answers in their science notebook.

1. DESCRIBE **How is the beaver changing where it lives?** (The beaver is cutting down trees, cutting them up into smaller pieces, and is going to use these to build a shelter. The beaver changes the forest by cutting down trees and it changes the river by building a dam in it, blocking the water from moving.)
2. EXPLAIN **Which animals are changing where they live to find food? Explain how these animals are changing their environment to meet their needs.** (The skunk is digging in the ground looking for food. It is changing the land by making holes in the ground. The woodpecker is drilling a hole in the tree to get food. It is changing the tree by making holes in it to get the food it needs to live. The woodpecker's beak is a part of it's body that is shaped to be able to make holes in trees, so that the woodpecker can meet its needs. It is part of the natural world that the woodpecker and tree work together to allow the woodpecker to eat.)

Teacher Rubric Use the scale descriptions to guide your assessment of the student's work. Assess each item separately, and then decide on one overall score, using the following scale:

4: Student performs with thorough understanding.
3: Student performs with adequate understanding.
2: Student performs with basic understanding.
1: Student performs with limited understanding.

Rubric	Scale			
The student worked with a partner to examine pictures in order to determine how living things change the places where they live.	4	3	2	1
The student worked with a partner to describe *why* living things change the places where they live.	4	3	2	1
The student shared ideas for how and why living things change the places where they live and listened to the ideas of others.	4	3	2	1
The student listened to others and revised conclusions based on ideas put forth by others.	4	3	2	1
Overall Score	4	3	2	1

Student Rubric Have students complete a self-evaluation similar to that shown below.

Rubric	Yes	Not Yet
1 I can work with a partner to closely observe pictures.		
2 I can work with a partner to describe how and why living things change the places where they live.		
3 I can share my ideas and listen to the ideas of others.		
4 I can change my ideas if I need to.		

People Use Resources

NEXT GENERATION SCIENCE STANDARDS | DISCIPLINARY CORE IDEAS
ESS3.A: Natural Resources Humans use natural resources for everything they do. (K-ESS3-1)

Objective Students will be able to:
- Explain that humans use natural resources for everything they do.

Science Vocabulary
resources

ENGAGE

Tap Prior Knowledge

- Discuss with the class what people need to live. Say: **People are living things.** Ask: **What do living things need to live?** (air, water, food, and shelter) Have students discuss how they meet their needs. For example, ask students to share the ways they can get food and water. (the supermarket, the refrigerator/pantry, the faucet) Then discuss how we all breathe the air around us. Ask: **What is your shelter?** (Students should say that their home, or where they live, is their shelter.) Make a list on chart paper of what people need and write the different ways students share that they meet these needs.

EXPLORE

Explore Natural Resources

- Invite students to look at the picture of the farm scene on pages 24–25. Ask: **What do you see growing in the ground?** (Sample answers: plants, vegetables, corn) **What might the tractor be doing?** Have students share ideas about what tractors do on a farm. Guide students to understand that tractors pull objects that harvest plants, till the ground for planting, and so on.
- Point to the small picture of the house on page 24. Ask: **What is happening in this picture?** Have students share their answers. Students may say that people are building a house. Students may also say that the house is being built with pieces of wood, and that it is not finished.

Set a Purpose and Read

- Tell students to listen to find out how and why people use natural resources.
- Have students follow along as you read aloud pages 24–25.

EXPLAIN

Define Resources

- Reread the main heading and text on pages 24–25, pointing to the word *resources* each time it is read. Say: **A natural *resource* is something from nature, or the environment, that people use.**
- Point to the house on page 24. Say: **This house is being built with wood. Wood comes from trees. Wood is a *resource* from nature that people use.** Point to the fields of crops in the farm scene. Say: **Different crops grow in these fields on the farm. Crops are the fruits and vegetables that people eat. They are a *resource* from nature that people use.** Ask: **What do the crops grow in?** Guide students to discover that the crops are growing in the ground and that soil also is a natural resource.

Explain How and Why People Use Resources From Nature

- Review with students again that people are living things that need air, water, food, and shelter. Ask: **Why do people build homes?** (They need shelter; they need a place to live.) **What resource from nature is being used to build this house?** (wood) **Where do people get this resource?** (from nature; from trees) **Why do you think some people use wood to build homes?** Discuss possible reasons for using wood, such as: It is easy to cut and shape to make things; it is strong and durable; there is a lot of it; and we can plant and grow more trees.
- Direct students to look at the picture of the farm scene. Ask: **What have farmers planted in these fields?** (plants; crops; fruits and vegetables) **What resources from nature do the plants need to grow?** (water, air, sunlight, and soil) **Why do farmers grow crops?** (so people can eat them; so they can pick them and sell them to other people for food; to make into other things for people to use) Discuss how the crops are a resource from nature that people

need in order to live. Ask: **Why do people need farmers to grow crops?** (People need food and cannot grow most things themselves; farmers grow the fruits, vegetables, and grains that people need to live.) Discuss that a farm is a place where there is plenty of space and soil to grow crops and that most people do not have these types of natural resources where they live. People rely on farmers to use natural resources to grow food for others.

ELABORATE

Find Out More About Natural Resources

Have students work in four groups to explore different resources from nature that people need. **Step 1:** Assign each group a human need—air, water, food, or shelter. Then have each group research how people use resources from nature to meet these needs. Provide illustrated books and Internet resources for groups to explore. Have groups draw pictures in their science notebook to represent what they discover.
Step 2: If time permits, invite groups to share their results with the class.

Extend Your Thinking About Trees

Ask students to think about the following: **How do people use trees as a resource? What needs can people meet using trees?** Discuss trees as a resource from nature that can be grown over and over again. This type of resources is called a *renewable resource*. Brainstorm different things that people make and do with trees. Record students' ideas on chart paper. Review the group list, identifying things that meet a human need (e.g., homes and fires to provide safe, warm shelter; fruits from trees to eat; seeds from trees to eat and plant to grow more fruits and more trees)

EVALUATE

Have students record the answer to the Wrap It Up question in their science notebook.

Wrap It Up!

1. CONCLUDE **How do people use resources to meet their needs?** (People use the wood from trees to build homes and shelters. Farmers use soil and water to grow crops. People eat the fruits, vegetables, and grains that farmers grow.)

SCIENCE BACKGROUND

Using Natural Resources

Resources from nature, or natural resources, are materials from Earth that meet human needs. Oil, natural gas, metals, stone, coal, and wood are some examples of natural resources. Air, sunlight, soil, and water are natural resources, as are animals, birds, fish, and plants. These natural resources are used to make food, fuel, and materials for producing other goods. All of the food that people eat comes from plants and animals. Coal, natural gas, and oil are used to produce heat, light, and power. We also make from natural resources everyday items such as clothing, cars, computers, and lunchboxes.

READING CONNECTION

Identify the Main Topic

With prompting and support, identify the main topic and retell key details of the text.

Guide students to identify the main topic and retell key details of the text. For example, in the EXPLORE section after reading the main heading, ask: **What do you think the main topic of this lesson is?** (Students should recognize that the lesson title tells the main topic—people use resources.) As you move through the EXPLAIN section, have students use details from the text to explain how people use wood to make buildings and soil to grow crops, all to meet human needs.

Using Resources Wisely

NEXT GENERATION SCIENCE STANDARDS | DISCIPLINARY CORE IDEAS
ESS3.C: Human Impacts on Earth Systems Things that people do to live comfortably can affect the world around them. But they can make choices that reduce their impacts on the land, water, air, and other living things. (K-ESS3-3)

Objectives **Students will be able to:**
- Explain how things that people do to live can affect the world around them.
- Identify choices that people can make that reduce their impacts on the land, water, air, and other living things.

Science Vocabulary
reuse

ENGAGE

Tap Prior Knowledge

- Ask students to think about ways they use resources from nature in their everyday lives. Say: **We use resources from nature every day. We use water to brush our teeth every morning and night and to take baths. We use electricity to keep our homes bright and warm. Electricity is made using different natural resources such as coal, wind, and even the sun.** Discuss with students how they can help conserve, or use lesser amounts of these resources from nature. Have students suggest ways that they can save resources at home.

EXPLORE

Preview the Lesson

- Display pages 26–27 and have students share what different things they observe.
- Point to the picture of the pile of tires on page 27. Ask: **What are these?** (old tires) **How do the tires look?** Have students share their opinions about how the tires look, discussing how they are probably old and worn out. Point to the picture of the playground. Ask: **What do you notice in this playground?** Have students describe everything they see.

Set a Purpose and Read

- Read the lesson title. Tell students to listen to find out how people can help save resources.
- Have students follow along as you read aloud pages 26–27.

EXPLAIN

Define Reuse

- Reread the text and captions on pages 26–27, pointing to the word *reuse* when it appears. Say: **When you *reuse* something, you use it more than one time.** Point to the picture of the pile of tires on page 26. Say: **These tires are old and worn out. They cannot be used on cars anymore.** Point to the surface of the playground. Say: **People can reuse the tires by using them again to make the ground beneath the playground safer for children.**
- Ask students to think about something that they can reuse. Discuss how they can make different things out of old food containers, such as oatmeal containers, deli containers, cans, and water bottles. Show some of these items to students, or show pictures of these items, and brainstorm different things that students could make using these reusable materials. (Possible suggestions: wind chime, bird feeder, drum, rattles/maracas, pencil holders)

Explain How People Can Save Resources

- Point to the lesson's main heading on page 26 and read it aloud again. Say: **When you use a resource wisely, you are using the resource in a way that doesn't waste it or overuse it.** Point to the picture of the pile of worn out tires. Ask: **Why are these tires not being used on cars?** (The tires are old and worn out; they do not work well as tires for cars anymore.) **How do you think they ended up in this pile?** (Possible answer: People threw them away because they didn't need them anymore.)
- Guide students to look at the picture of the playground surface. Read the caption text aloud. Say: **How do you think this surface was made?** (People broke up old tires into small pieces; people used a machine to crush up the worn-out tires to make it.) **What do you think this surface feels like?** (bouncy, soft, crumbly) Explain to students that tires are made of rubber, which is a resource from nature. Rubber is springy and soft. **Why is this a good surface for**

a playground? (It is softer than the ground; it is springy and not hard, so children can stay safe on the playground.) **Why is it important to reuse things?** (Possible answer: If we throw away everything we use, we will run out of places to put the trash. If we reuse things, we can save resources.)

- Ask: **How can people use resources from nature wisely?** (Possible answers: reusing things instead of throwing them away; using less of things such as water; finding new uses for old things)

ELABORATE

Extend Your Thinking About Resources

My science notebook

Say: **Some natural resources will always be here, such as air, water, and sunlight. There are other natural resources that may run out if we do not use them wisely.** Ask: **What resources can run out?** Write a list of student's ideas on chart paper. Then provide small groups of students with research materials such as illustrated books, magazines, and Internet access to find answers to this question. Explain that a renewable resource is one that can grow back or will not run out, such as wind, sunlight, air, water, and trees. Nonrenewable resources are resources from nature that people use faster than they are made in nature, such as oil, natural gas, and coal. If we use too much of these resources, we could run out and they would be gone forever. Remind students, however, that we should use ALL resources wisely, so that all living things have clean air, water, and space to live and grow.

EVALUATE

My science notebook

Have students record the answer to the Wrap It Up question in their science notebook.

Wrap It Up!

1. APPLY **How can you reuse something old in a new way instead of throwing it in the trash?** (Possible answers: I can reuse food containers to make drums or other instruments; I can reuse paper cups so that I don't have to use a new one every time I want a drink of water; I can reuse paper by drawing on both sides and saving scraps to use for other art projects.)

ELL SUPPORT

Reusing Resources

Beginning Point to the pile of tires. Ask: **Are these tires made from reused materials?** (No.) **Can people reuse these tires to make something else?** (Yes.) Point to the playground surface. **Is this playground surface made from reused materials?** (Yes.) **What was reused to make this surface?** (old tires)

Intermediate Provide sentence frames to help students describe how people can reuse resources: *Tires can be (reused) to make something else. A playground surface can be made from (reused) tires.*

Advanced Ask students to draw a picture showing different ways that people can reuse materials to make something new. Work with students to help write descriptive words about the new creation and what resource was reused to make it.

READING CONNECTION

Understand Unknown Words

With prompting and support, ask and answer questions about unknown words in a text.

Guide students to ask and answer questions about unknown words in a text. For example, in the EXPLAIN section reread the main heading. Point out the word *wisely*. Say: **This may be an unfamiliar word. We can ask ourselves a question about this word and then look for clues to its meaning in the text and pictures. First, I notice that *wisely* includes the word *wise*. What does *wise* mean?** (smart; using good judgement) **Knowing what *wise* means helps me figure out that *wisely* means "being smart or using good judgement about something." Look at the pictures. Why was reusing the tires a wise thing to do?** (Possible answer: The playground needed a soft surface underneath it so if children fall, they do not get hurt.)

Share Solutions

NEXT GENERATION SCIENCE STANDARDS | PERFORMANCE EXPECTATION

K-ESS3-3. Communicate solutions that will reduce the impact of humans on the land, water, air, and/or other living things in the local environment. [Clarification Statement: Examples of human impact on the land could include cutting trees to produce paper and using resources to produce bottles. Examples of solutions could include reusing paper and recycling cans and bottles.]

K–2 ETS1-2. Develop a simple sketch, drawing, or physical model to illustrate how the shape of an object helps it function as needed to solve a given problem.

NEXT GENERATION SCIENCE STANDARDS | DISCIPLINARY CORE IDEAS

ETS1.B: Designs can be conveyed through sketches, drawings or physical models. These representations are useful in communicating ideas for a problem's solutions to other people. *(K-2-ETS1-2, secondary to K-ESS-3)*

Objective **Students will be able to:**

- Communicate solutions that will reduce the impact of humans on the land, water, air, and/or other living things in the local environment.

CLASSROOM MANAGEMENT

Suggested Materials provide a variety of drawing and writing materials such as pencils, colored pencils, markers, crayons, white paper

Time 5 minutes for planning; 15 minutes for drawing; 15 minutes for sharing

Teaching Tips Review with students the different resources from nature that they learned about in previous lessons and how people can reuse these resources to make something new. It might be useful to have a class brainstorming session to generate a list on chart paper of natural resources we use every day, such as air, water, sunlight, soil, wood, and so on.

What to Expect Students should think of a plan in which they can reuse a resource in a different way, helping the environment by reducing the amount of things they throw away, thereby using less of a resource that we need to conserve. By doing this, students should understand and communicate how they are reducing their impact on the land, water, air, and/or other living things around them.

ENGAGE

Set the scene.

- Read the introductory text on page 28 aloud. Say: **A resource is something you use, such as water and air. We also use resources to make things that we can then use, such as wooden pencils or cotton socks.** Discuss with students the different resources that they use every day, either raw (used unchanged, such as water and air) or in a changed state (made into something we use such as a pencil or piece of paper).
- Explain that in this lesson, students will be thinking of how they can use a resource in a new way. Pont out the pictures on page 29. Say: **These pictures show a way to reuse socks to make sock puppets.** Ask: **Can you think of another way to reuse socks?** Have students suggest their ideas.

Define a problem.

- Read aloud the question from the introductory text: *What can you do to help the environment?* Explain that the *environment* is everything around us including the land, air, water, and all living things—plants, animals, and humans. Discuss that when we reuse resources, we are helping our environment by reducing the amount of things we throw away. We are also using less of a resource if we reuse our old things or make something new with them.

EXPLORE

Think of an idea.

- Read step 1 aloud. Use questions such as those that follow to guide students as they think of a new way of using a resource. Ask:
  - **What do you have at home that you might only use for a short while and then throw away?**
  - **How can you use any of these things in a different way?**
  - **What do you use every day that you could use less of or use in a new way?**
  - **How will you be helping the environment by doing this?**
  - **How are some of these things that can be used again, or in a different way, similar?**
- Help groups having difficulty with ideas by asking more pointed questions, such as:
  - **How could you use less water by using it differently?**
  - **How could you reuse paper?**
  - **How could you reuse empty cans, bottles, or other containers?**
- Examples of student ideas might include ways to conserve water, ways to reuse old clothing or toys, ways to reuse paper or scraps, or ways to reuse empty cans, bottles, or other containers.
- You may wish to pair students and have partners discuss their ideas. Encourage partners to give each other feedback as to how well the ideas might work, improvements they might make, and other ideas they might consider.

SCIENCE AND ENGINEERING PRACTICES

Obtaining, Evaluating, and Communicating Information

- Say: **Engineers communicate solutions with others in oral and/or written forms using models and/or drawings that provide detail about scientific ideas.** In this activity, students drew pictures of different ways they can reduce the impact of humans on the environment. Ask: **What are other ways that you could communicate the idea that you drew for this activity?** (Possible answers: I could make a model, I could make a video, I could write about my idea.)

Developing and Using Models

- In this activity, students made drawings to communicate their ideas. Discuss with students that drawings are models. Ask: **What other times have you made models to represent events or design solutions?** (Possible answers: I observed the sun on a sunny day and drew a model representing how it appeared to rise in the morning. I observed my friend sliding down a slide and drew a model representing how my friend was moving.)

CROSSCUTTING CONCEPTS

Cause and Effect

- Say: **Engineers know that events have causes that generate observable patterns.** Ask: **What is an observable pattern you can make when you recycle things you use everyday?** (I can observe that my family makes less trash when we recycle.)
- Encourage students to link the concept of cause and effect to other science lessons. For example in physical science pushes and pulls can make objects start and stop moving

Structure and Function

- Discuss with students how they can observe that the shape and structure of objects are related to their function. For example a sock is designed to be soft and flexible so that it can fit on a foot. Or be reused as a puppet.
- Encourage students to link concepts of structure and function to other science lessons. For example a beaver has specially shaped teeth to cut into trees

Share Solutions (continued)

EXPLORE (continued)

Draw a picture.

My science notebook Read step 2 aloud. Have students draw a picture of their idea in their science notebook. Encourage students to include as many details as they can in their drawings. Assist students with writing words or a sentence describing their pictures.

EXPLAIN

Share your drawings.

- Again pair students, and have them share their drawings with each other. Encourage students to explain the materials they will be using, what they will do with the materials, and how this reuse of materials will help the environment.
- Say: **After your partner tells you about their solution for helping the environment, provide feedback. *Feedback* includes reactions to and comments about an idea. When you give feedback, you need to give it in a positive way. First tell your partner what you like about the idea. Then make any suggestions you have for making it better.**
- Have students switch roles and repeat. Then say: **Take a few moments and revise your ideas based on your partner's feedback.**
- When students are satisfied with their revised solution, have them explain how they came up with their ideas, what they will be conserving or reusing, and how this solution can help the environment. Then have students try out their ideas at home. Ask students for reactions and comments from others at home about their ideas. Then ask students to revise their ideas in order to make them better. Encourage students to draw pictures or write words or sentences about their revised plan and tell how it worked. (Example student explanation: Many people in my family drink water from plastic bottles. They don't always finish the water in the bottles. My plan was to have the people in my family pour all the leftover water into a bucket. All of the people in my family tried my plan. When the bucket was full of water, we used it to water plants inside and outside our home. My plan was also to place the used plastic bottles into a recycling bin. This plan worked well with my family. When I asked my family what they liked and did not like about my ideas, they came up with more ideas. They liked what we did. They thought we could do more by reusing some of the bottles. We decided to cut off the tops of the bottles, fill the bottoms with soil, and use them as pots for plants. All of these solutions will help the environment.)
- Ask: **In what ways did you think like an engineer as you completed this activity?** (I brainstormed solutions to an important problem. Then I made a drawing and shared it with my partner. Engineers do this too. Then they test their ideas to see how well they work.)

ELABORATE

- Have students focus on recycling as another way that they can help the environment.
Step 1: Help students research different materials that can be recycled at a recycling drop-off location or through local recycling collection. (paper, plastic bottles, cans, glass, used wood)
Step 2: Help students choose a recyclable material, and then research the different things that this resource can be made into (e.g., old newspapers into new newspapers; old paper into notepaper or cards; old bottles and cans into new plastic and metal containers; old scraps of wood into new wooden materials such as furniture or floors for homes). Have students draw a picture of their recycled resource.
Step 3: If time permits, encourage students to share with the class how recycling their resource will help the environment.

EVALUATE

Check to make sure that students have recorded their solution to help the environment in their science notebook. Then ask students these questions. Have them record the answers in their science notebook.

1. **LIST What are some ways we can use resources again?** (We can recycle cans, bottles, and newspapers. We can make new things from old, used things.)
2. **APPLY How can using resources in a different way help the environment?** (If you reuse or use fewer resources from nature, then there will be plenty of these resources for everyone and we will not run out. If you reuse resources instead of throwing them away, there will be less trash on the land and more places for plants and animals to live.)

RUBRICS

Teacher Rubric Use the scale descriptions to guide your assessment of the student's work. Assess each item separately, and then decide on one overall score, using the following scale:

4: Student performs with thorough understanding.
3: Student performs with adequate understanding.
2: Student performs with basic understanding.
1: Student performs with limited understanding.

Rubric	Scale			
The student thought of an idea and planned how to represent the idea to answer the question.	4	3	2	1
The student showed a way to reuse resources effectively.	4	3	2	1
The student effectively explained his/her idea, listened to constructive feedback, and made revisions.	4	3	2	1
The student communicated ideas pictorially and verbally, including explanations that conveyed how his/her idea can help the environment.	4	3	2	1
Overall Score	4	3	2	1

Student Rubric Have students complete a self-evaluation similar to that shown below.

Rubric	Yes	Not Yet
1 I can think of new way of using resources in order to answer the question asked.		
2 I can make a drawing to show my idea.		
3 I can explain my result, listen to feedback, and revise my idea.		
4 I can communicate results, explaining how my idea can help the environment.		
Overall Score		

NATIONAL GEOGRAPHIC LEARNING | Science Career

Wildlife Expert

NEXT GENERATION SCIENCE STANDARDS | CONNECTION TO NATURE OF SCIENCE
Scientific Knowledge Is Based on Empirical Evidence Scientists look for patterns and order when making observations about the world.

Objective **Students will be able to:**
- Understand how scientists such as wildlife experts look for patterns and order when making observations about the world.

ENGAGE

Tap Prior Knowledge

- Invite students to discuss farm animals that they have seen at a farm or in books. Talk about how a farmer's job is to care for his animals as a parent cares for a child. Ask: **What might farmers do to take care of their animals?** (Answers should include providing food, water, and a safe place to live, or shelter.) Discuss how a farmer also needs to protect his animals from danger.

EXPLORE

Explore Protecting Wildlife

- Show page 30 to students. Ask: **What do you see in this picture? What is the man holding? Why do you think he is holding the goat?**
- Have students share their answers. Some students may say that they see a man holding an animal in his coat. Some students may be able to identify that the animal is a baby goat. Students may suggest that the man is protecting the goat, keeping it warm and safe.

Set a Purpose and Read

- Read the main heading aloud. Tell students to listen as you read aloud the text to find out about an Explorer who is a wildlife expert.
- Have students follow along as you read aloud page 30.

EXPLAIN

Describe the Work of an Explorer Who Is a Wildlife Expert

- Reread aloud again page 30. Say: **Shafqat Hussain is a wildlife expert. Shafqat Hussain traveled to the Himalayan Mountains to study the people and wildlife living there. Snow leopards and goat farmers live in the Himalayan Mountains.** If possible, show students a map of the world, pointing to the location of the Himalayas and to your location.
- Point to the picture of the man on page 30. Ask: **What does Shafqat Hussain do?** (He is a wildlife expert who works to protect snow leopards.) Explain that *wildlife* is any animal that lives in the wild, and that an *expert* is anyone who knows a great deal about something. Ask: **How does Shafqat Hussain protect snow leopards?** (He talks to farmers; he finds ways to keep the farmers from killing the snow leopards.)

Connect Science Topics to the Work of an Explorer

- Say: **We have been learning about how people can help the environment. The environment is all the living and nonliving things around us.** Ask: **What are some ways that we can help protect the environment where we live? Student's answers may include different ways to reuse/recycle resources so that we do not use up the resources and so that we can be more careful with the air, land, water, and living things around us.**
- Ask: **How does Shafqat Hussain help protect living things in this environment?** (He protects snow leopards; he finds ways to keep farmers from killing the snow leopards.) **Why do the farmers want to kill the snow leopards?** (Snow leopards sometimes hunt farmers' goats. Killing the snow leopards helps keep the goats safe.)

- Ask: **What might happen if the snow leopards are killed?** (Possible answer: There will be no more snow leopards left.) **Why is Shafqat Hussain's work important?** (Possible answer: He is helping to make sure that the snow leopards can continue to live.)

Find Out More

- Ask: **Is a wildlife expert's job interesting to you? Why or why not?** (Allow students to share their answers. Accept all positive and negative responses.) For students who find this to be an interesting career, ask: **Why would you like to be a wildlife expert?** (Possible answer: I would like to be wildlife expert because I love animals and want to help them.)

ELABORATE

Find Out More About Snow Leopards

My science notebook

Help students research about snow leopards. Provide illustrated books and/or Internet resources for students to use. Invite students to discover what these animals look like, where they live, and what they eat. Encourage students to explore why these animals are considered "endangered," or disappearing from Earth as they are being killed by people. Have students draw a picture in their science notebook. Provide assistance with writing text about snow leopards.

EVALUATE

My science notebook

Ask students these questions. Have them record their answers in their science notebook.

1. **EXPLAIN How does Shafqat Hussain help protect snow leopards?** (He talks to farmers and finds ways to keep the farmers from killing the snow leopards.)
2. **INFER How can wildlife experts help living things?** (They can work to protect living things by talking to others about what they know to solve problems and stop others from destroying these living things.)

READING CONNECTION

Identify the Main Topic

With prompting and support, identify the main topic and retell key details of a text.

Guide students as they identify the main topic and retell key details of a text. For example, as you preview the lesson with students, point out the heading at the top of the page (Science Career). Ask: **What will we be learning about in this lesson?** (a science career) Then read the heading in the black lozenge and the first sentence of text. Ask: **What does this text tell you?** (It tells you that this lesson is about an explorer who is a wildlife expert.) In the EXPLAIN section when asking students to connect science topics to the work of an explorer, have students use key details from the text to tell what Shafqat Hussain does to protect living things.

Test Administration Script for DCI Review: Life Science

For Questions 1–10

SAY: You are going to take a short test about plants and animals. Listen to the directions. (Hold up a page and point.) For each question, you will look at the pictures and listen to a question. Then you will circle one picture to mark your answer. Before you start, are there any questions? (Pause.)

1. Find number 1. Circle the picture that shows a living thing. (ESS3.A)
2. Find number 2. Circle the picture that shows something that needs light to live. (LS1.C)
3. Find number 3. Circle the picture that shows something humans made using a resource from nature. (ESS3.A)
4. Find number 4. Circle the picture that shows a plant getting the water it needs. (LS1.C)
5. Find number 5. Circle the picture that shows an animal in its shelter. (ESS3.A)
6. Find number 6. Circle the picture that shows a resource that can be reused to make the surface of a playground. (ESS3.C)
7. Find number 7. Circle the picture that shows how a tree's roots can change the place where it lives. (ESS2.E)
8. Find number 8. Circle the picture that shows how an animal digging a shelter can change the place where it lives. (ESS2.E)
9. Find number 9. Circle the picture that shows an animal eating another animal for food. (LS1.C)
10. Find number 10. Circle the picture that shows an animal getting the water it needs where it lives. (ESS3.A)

Name ______________________________

DCI Review: Life Science

1

A

B

C

2

A

B

C

3

A

B

C

4

A

B

C

Name ____________________

5

A

B

C

6

A

B

C

7

A

B

C

Name ______

8

A

B

C

9

A

B

C

10

A

B

C

Pauta para tomar la prueba para el repaso de las IDB: Ciencias de la vida

Para las preguntas 1 a 10

DIGA: Van a dar una prueba corta sobre las plantas y los animales. Escuchen las instrucciones. (Muestre una página y señálela). Para cada pregunta, mirarán los dibujos y escucharán una pregunta. Luego, encerrarán su respuesta en un círculo. Antes de comenzar, ¿tienen alguna duda? (Haga una pausa).

1. Hallen el número 1. Encierren en un círculo el dibujo que muestra un ser vivo. (ESS3.A)

2. Hallen el número 2. Encierren en un círculo el dibujo que muestra algo que necesita luz para vivir. (LS1.C)

3. Hallen el número 3. Encierren en un círculo el dibujo que muestra algo que hicieron los seres humanos con un recurso de la naturaleza. (ESS3.A)

4. Hallen el número 4. Encierren en un círculo el dibujo que muestra una planta que recibe el agua que necesita. (LS1.C)

5. Hallen el número 5. Encierren en un círculo el dibujo que muestra un animal en su refugio. (ESS3.A)

6. Hallen el número 6. Encierren en un círculo el dibujo que muestra un recurso que pueda reutilizarse para hacer la superficie de un patio de juegos. (ESS3.C)

7. Hallen el número 7. Encierren en un círculo el dibujo que muestra cómo las raíces de un árbol pueden cambiar el lugar donde vive. (ESS2.E)

8. Hallen el número 8. Encierren en un círculo el dibujo que muestra cómo un animal que cava un refugio puede cambiar el lugar donde vive. (ESS2.E)

9. Hallen el número 9. Encierren en un círculo el dibujo que muestra un animal que se alimenta de otros animales. (LS1.C)

10. Hallen el número 10. Encierren en un círculo el dibujo que muestra un animal que obtiene el agua que necesita donde vive. (ESS3.A)

Nombre ____________________

Repaso de las IDB: Ciencias de la vida

1

A

B

C

2

A

B

C

3

A

B

C

4

A

B

C

Nombre ____

5

A

B

C

6

A

B

C

7

A

B

C

Nombre ____________________

8

A

B

C

9

A

B

C

10

A

B

C

DCI Review Answer Key for Life Science

LIFE SCIENCE

K. Interdependent Relationships in Ecosystems: Animals, Plants, and Their Environment

Question Number	Answer
1	C
2	A
3	B
4	C
5	C
6	A
7	A
8	B
9	A
10	C

NOTES

Earth Science

Grade K. Weather and Climate

Performance Expectations

Students who demonstrate understanding can:

K-PS3-1. Make observations to determine the effect of sunlight on Earth's surface. [Clarification Statement: Examples of Earth's surface could include sand, soil, rocks, and water] [*Assessment Boundary: Assessment of temperature is limited to relative measures such as warmer/cooler.*]

K-PS3-2. Use tools and materials to design and build a structure that will reduce the warming effect of sunlight on an area. [Clarification Statement: Examples of structures could include umbrellas, canopies, and tents that minimize the warming effect of the sun.]

K-ESS2-1. Use and share observations of local weather conditions to describe patterns over time. [Clarification Statement: Examples of qualitative observations could include descriptions of the weather (such as sunny, cloudy, rainy, and warm); examples of quantitative observations could include numbers of sunny, windy, and rainy days in a month. Examples of patterns could include that it is usually cooler in the morning than in the afternoon and the number of sunny days versus cloudy days in different months.] [*Assessment Boundary: Assessment of quantitative observations limited to whole numbers and relative measures such as warmer/cooler.*]

K-ESS3-2. Ask questions to obtain information about the purpose of weather forecasting to prepare for, and respond to, severe weather. [Clarification Statement: Emphasis is on local forms of severe weather.]

Disciplinary Core Ideas

PS3.B: Conservation of Energy and Energy Transfer

- Sunlight warms Earth's surface. (K-PS3-1), (K-PS3-2)

ESS2.D: Weather and Climate

- Weather is the combination of sunlight, wind, snow or rain, and temperature in a particular region at a particular time. People measure these conditions to describe and record the weather and to notice patterns over time. (K-ESS2-1)

ESS3.B: Natural Hazards

- Some kinds of severe weather are more likely than others in a given region. Weather scientists forecast severe weather so that the communities can prepare for and respond to these events. (K-ESS3-2)

ETS1.A: Defining and Delimiting an Engineering Problem

- Asking questions, making observations, and gathering information are helpful in thinking about problems. *(secondary to K-ESS3-2)*

Science and Engineering Practices

Planning and Carrying Out Investigations

Planning and carrying out investigations to answer questions or test solutions to problems in K–2 builds on prior experiences and progresses to simple investigations, based on fair tests, which provide data to support explanations or design solutions.

- Make observations (firsthand or from media) to collect data that can be used to make comparisons. (K-PS3-1)

Constructing Explanations and Designing Solutions
Constructing explanations and designing solutions in K–2 builds on prior experiences and progresses to the use of evidence and ideas in constructing evidence-based accounts of natural phenomena and designing solutions.

- Use tools and materials provided to design and build a device that solves a specific problem or a solution to a specific problem. (K-PS3-2)

Analyzing and Interpreting Data
Analyzing data in K–2 builds on prior experiences and progresses to collecting, recording, and sharing observations.

- Use observations (firsthand or from media) to describe patterns in the natural world in order to answer scientific questions. (K-ESS2-1)

Asking Questions and Defining Problems
Asking questions and defining problems in grades K–2 builds on prior experiences and progresses to simple descriptive questions that can be tested.

- Ask questions based on observations to find more information about the designed world. (K-ESS3-2)

Obtaining, Evaluating, and Communicating Information
Obtaining, evaluating, and communicating information in K–2 builds on prior experiences and uses observations and texts to communicate new information.

- Read grade-appropriate texts and/or use media to obtain scientific information to describe patterns in the natural world. (K-ESS3-2)

Crosscutting Concepts

Cause and Effect

- Events have causes that generate observable patterns. (K-PS3-1), (K-PS3-2), (K-ESS3-2)

Patterns

- Patterns in the natural world can be observed, used to describe phenomena, and used as evidence. (K-ESS2-1)

Connections to Nature of Science
Scientific Investigations Use a Variety of Methods

- Scientists use different ways to study the world. (K-PS3-1)

Science Knowledge is Based on Empirical Evidence

- Scientists look for patterns and order when making observations about the world. (K-ESS2-1)

Connections to Engineering, Technology, and Applications of Science
Interdependence of Science, Engineering, and Technology

- People encounter questions about the natural world every day. (K-ESS3-2)

Influence of Engineering, Technology, and Science on Society and the Natural World

- People depend on various technologies in their lives; human life would be very different without technology. (K-ESS3-2)

K-2-ETS1 Engineering Design

K-2-ETS1-1. Ask questions, make observations, and gather information about a situation people want to change to define a simple problem that can be solved through the development of a new or improved object or tool.

Disciplinary Core Ideas

ETS1.A: Defining and Delimiting an Engineering Problem

- Asking questions, making observations, and gathering information are helpful in thinking about problems. (K-2-ETS1-1)

Science and Engineering Practices
Asking Questions and Defining Problems
Asking questions and defining problems in K–2 builds on prior experiences and progresses to simple descriptive questions.

- Ask questions based on observations to find more information about the natural and/or designed world(s). (K-2-ETS1-1)
- Define a simple problem that can be solved through the development of a new or improved object or tool. (K-2-ETS1-1)

The Sun Warms Earth

NEXT GENERATION SCIENCE STANDARDS | DISCIPLINARY CORE IDEAS
PS3.B: Conservation of Energy and Energy Transfer Sunlight warms Earth's surface. (K-PS3-1), (K-PS3-2)

Objective **Students will be able to:**

- Identify the sun as the object that warms Earth's land, water, and air.

ENGAGE

Tap Prior Knowledge

- Ask students to think about a warm, sunny day. Say: **Think about being outside on a bright, sunny day. Then think about facing the sun and closing your eyes.** Ask: **How does your face feel when the sun is shining on it?** (Possible answer: warm)

EXPLORE

Preview the Lesson

- Have students observe the picture on pages 4–5. Ask: **What do you see in this picture?** (Possible answers: I see a lot of houses close together. I see cliffs made of rock. I see some green plants. I see water and boats. I see clouds and the sun in the sky.) **How can you tell that the sun is shining?** (Possible answers: I see shadows on the houses. I see a bright spot in the sky, and that's the sun.)
- Read aloud the lesson's main heading. Explain that Earth is the planet we live on. Ask: **What does the title of this lesson tell you about the sun?** (The lesson title tells me that the sun warms our planet.)

Set a Purpose and Read

- Tell students to listen to find what things on Earth are warmed by the sun's energy.
- Have students follow along as you read aloud pages 4–5.

EXPLAIN

Identify What Things on Earth the Sun's Energy Warms

- After you read pages 4–5, have students look for key details by asking: **What words in the text name things on Earth that are warmed by sunlight?** (*skin, water, land, air*) Direct students to study the picture on pages 4–5. Ask: **What things in the picture are being warmed by sunlight?** (Possible answers: Sunlight warms houses, buildings, plants, steps, porches, rocky cliffs, the water, and boats.)
- Have a volunteer point to a sunny place in the picture. Ask: **How would you feel in that sunny place?** (Possible answers: I would feel warm or hot. My eyes might hurt from the bright light.) **What else in that sunny place would feel warm?** (Possible answer: The building/wall/road would feel warm, too.)
- Have another volunteer point to a shady place. Ask: **How would you feel in that shady place?** (Possible answers: I would feel cooler than in the sun. It would not be as bright in the shade.)
- Read aloud the caption on page 5. Ask: **What do you think would happen if sunlight did not warm Earth?** (Possible answer: Earth would be very cold.) **Why is the sun important?** (Possible answer: The sun gives Earth light and keeps Earth warm.)

ELABORATE

Find Out More About Sunlight Warming Earth

My science notebook Have students find a sunny spot in or around the school building. Ask them to stand in the sunny spot and describe how they feel. Then have students find a shady spot. Ask them to stand in the shady spot and describe how they feel. Have students compare and contrast the relative warmth of the two spots.

Extend Your Thinking About Sunlight Warming Earth

My science notebook Have students use crayon shavings to demonstrate how sunlight warms Earth. Have small groups of students place a sheet of light-colored paper in a sunny spot. Have students sprinkle the crayon shavings on the paper. Ask students to predict what will happen to the shavings while they're in the sunlight. After three hours, have students check the crayon shavings. Have students record their predictions and observations in their science notebook in words or drawings. Ask: **What happened to the crayon shavings?** (They melted.) **What caused them to melt?** (The sunlight warmed them.)

EVALUATE

My science notebook Have students record the answer to the Wrap It Up question in their science notebook.

Wrap It Up!

1. RECALL **What does the sun do for the land?** (The sun lights and warms the land.)

TEACHING WITH TECHNOLOGY

Identify Things on Earth That the Sun Warms

Project the lesson on a whiteboard. Read aloud the last sentence: **The sun warms the water, land, and air, too.** Ask a volunteer to point to water in the picture. Then write the word *water* on the water. Repeat this activity for *land* and *air*. Ask volunteers to find other places in the picture that the sun warms. (houses, plants, steps, porches, cliffs, and boats) Draw a sun on each place. Read aloud the caption: **The sun warms everything in this picture.**

READING CONNECTION

Retell Key Details

With prompting and support, ask and answer questions about key details in a text.

Guide students to ask and answer questions as they read to help them identify and understand key details in the text. For example, in the ENGAGE section before you set a purpose for reading, point out and read the main heading. Challenge students to look at the picture and the heading and think of questions they have about the sun warming Earth. Have students listen for the answers to the questions as you read. Then in the EXPLAIN section have students discuss how the details in the text helped them answer their questions.

Investigate

Warmth from the Sun

NEXT GENERATION SCIENCE STANDARDS | PERFORMANCE EXPECTATION

K-PS3-1. Make observations to determine the effect of sunlight on Earth's surface. [Clarification Statement: Examples of Earth's surface could include sand, soil, rocks, and water] [*Assessment Boundary: Assessment of temperature is limited to relative measures such as warmer/cooler.*]

Objective **Students will be able to:**

- Evaluate the effect of sunlight on soil, sand, rocks, and water.

CLASSROOM MANAGEMENT

Materials ***For groups of 4:*** 2 cups of soil; 2 cups of sand; 2 cups of rocks; 2 cups of water ***For teacher use:*** 40 plastic cups (10 oz. size); soil (7½ cups); sand (7½ cups); rocks (7½ cups); water (7½ cups); masking tape; marker; measuring cup ***If doing the* Investigate *as a whole class activity, you will need:*** 8 plastic cups (10 oz. size); soil (1½ cups); sand (1½ cups); rocks (1½ cups); water (1½ cups); masking tape; marker; measuring cup

Time 20 minutes for setup; 15 minutes for observation

Advance Preparation Use masking tape and a marker to label each plastic cup to indicate what it will contain and whether it will be placed in the sun or the shade. Fill each plastic cup with ¾ cup soil, sand, rocks, or water. In order to control variables, be sure that all cups contain the same amount of material. Locate a sunny area and a shady area inside or outside the school where students can put their cups and the cups will not be disturbed. Choose areas that will remain in the sun or shade for the length of the investigation.

Teaching Tips Be sure the soil, sand, rocks, and water are cool before starting the investigation. Clarify for students the meaning of the words *warm* and *cool*. You may wish to have students touch a warm object and a cool object and compare how they feel. Use a whiteboard to model for students how to record observations in the data table. When handling the cups, model lab safety by wearing your safety goggles.

What to Expect Students will observe that the materials in the cups in the sunlight feel warmer after one hour than at the start of the investigation. They may notice that the water warmed less than the soil, sand, or rocks, as water absorbs heat energy more slowly than other materials. Students will also observe that the materials in the cups in the shade still feel cooler after one hour than the cups in the sun. Students will identify sunlight as the cause of the relative warmth of the materials in the sun-exposed cups.

ENGAGE

Tap Prior Knowledge

- Display the picture on pages 4–5. Have students use that picture to review the things on Earth that the sun warms. (The sun warms the land, water, and air.)

EXPLORE

- Have students wear safety goggles.
- Guide students through the investigation. Read pages 6–7 together.

My science notebook Help students construct a table for recording their observations in their science notebook, or project a table on a whiteboard and use it to record observations with the class. Example:

Warm or Cool?		
Earth Material	**Before**	**After**
soil; sun		
soil; shade		
sand; sun		
sand; shade		
rocks; sun		
rocks; shade		
water; sun		
water; shade		

- Before students do steps 1–4, write the words *soil*, *sand*, *rocks*, and *water* on the board. Clarify that these materials are part of Earth's surface.
- After one hour, have students observe the materials again by touching the materials, and record their observations in the data table in their science notebook.

EXPLAIN

- Have students share their observations with other groups. Ask: **How did the soil in both cups feel before the investigation?** (The soil in both cups felt cool.) **How did the soil in the sunny cup feel after one hour?** (It felt warm.) **How did the soil in the shady cup feel after one hour?** (cool.) Repeat this discussion about the cups of sand, rocks, and water.
- To help students establish evidence for their observations, ask: **How did you know if the soil, sand, rocks, or water were cool or warm?** (I felt them with my hand.)
- Ask probing questions to help students draw conclusions. For example, ask: **Why did the soil in the sunny cup feel warm after one hour?** (Possible answer: The soil was in the sun, and the sun warmed it.) **Why did the soil in the shady cup still feel cool after one hour?** (The sun did not shine on the soil in the shady cup, so that soil did not get as warm.)
- Ask: **How does the sun warm Earth's surface?** (by shining light on it)

ELABORATE

- Have students repeat their observations that the sun warms Earth's surface referencing common objects in the environment. For example, students can feel the surface of a sidewalk on the sunny side and on the shady side of the school. They should do this in the early morning before the sun has warmed either sidewalk. Later in the day, they can feel the same surfaces in the sun and in the shade.

EVALUATE

My science notebook

Check that students have recorded their observations in their science notebook. Have students record the answer to the Wrap It Up question in their science notebook as well.

Wrap It Up!

1. EVALUATE **How did sunlight change what was in the cups?** (The materials in the cups in the sunlight got warmer; the materials in the cups in the shade stayed cool.)

SCIENCE AND ENGINEERING PRACTICES

Planning and Carrying Out Investigations

- In this activity, students apply scientific ideas to plan and carry out an investigation. They use their sense of touch to make observations about whether the soil and sand are warm or cool. Ask students if they can think of other ways to find out if something is warm or cool. (Possible answer: I could use a thermometer.)

Connections to Nature of Science
Scientific Investigations Use a Variety of Methods

- Discuss with students how scientists may use different ways to make observations. They may use their senses and they may use tools to try to answer questions.

CROSSCUTTING CONCEPTS

Cause and Effect

- Discuss with students how events have causes that they can observe. In this activity they observed that sunlight warms their cups of materials. Ask students if they can think of other areas of science in which they can observe a cause and effect relationship. One example in physical science may be that if they push a door, it opens. Ask students to give other examples of cause and effect.

NATIONAL GEOGRAPHIC LEARNING | Think Like an Engineer

Design a Structure

NEXT GENERATION SCIENCE STANDARDS | PERFORMANCE EXPECTATION

K-PS3-2. Use tools and materials to design and build a structure that will reduce the warming effect of sunlight on an area. [Clarification Statement: Examples of structures could include umbrellas, canopies, and tents that minimize the warming effect of the sun.]

Objective **Students will be able to:**

- Work with a group to design and build a structure that will reduce the warming effect of sunlight on an area.

CLASSROOM MANAGEMENT

Suggested Materials ***For groups of 4:*** Assemble a variety of materials from which students can choose, including modeling clay; cloth; construction paper; cardboard; small dowels; craft sticks; pipe cleaners; tape; glue. You may wish to challenge students by also providing materials that will not block sunlight, such as tissue paper or clear plastic.

Time 10 minutes for planning; 15 minutes for building; 10 minutes for testing; 5 minutes for revising; 10 minutes for sharing

Advance Preparation Assemble all of the materials where students can see and use them. Provide trays or squares of corrugated cardboard on which groups can carry materials to their work area and that they can use as a base for their structure. Identify a sunny spot, preferably in a grassy area, where students can test the structures they design. A grassy area will transfer less heat to the bottom of the tray than an area that is made of asphalt or concrete. To reduce heat transfer that is not the result of the sun shining on the structures, is best if the testing site can be shaded prior to having students perform their tests. The structures should be left undisturbed in the sun for a least one hour.

Teaching Tips In order to meet the performance expectation, student groups must design their structures and conduct their tests by themselves. Coach students through the planning process without instructing them on specific steps to take or materials to use.

What to Expect Students will apply their understanding that sunlight warms Earth's surface, but shade keeps an area cool. They will use opaque materials to block sunlight, creating a shady area that is cool. Students will be able to share how they made their structure and describe how well it blocks sunlight.

ENGAGE

Set the scene.

- Have students recall the investigation in the previous lesson. Ask: **How did sunlight change the materials in the cups that were in a sunny place?** (Sunlight warmed the materials.) **What happened to the materials in the cups that were in a shady place?** (The materials stayed cool.)
- Read page 8 aloud as students look at the picture. Ask: **Which places on this beach are warm?** (The sunny places are warm.) **Which places on this beach are cooler?** (The shady places are cooler.) **Why do they stay cooler?** (The umbrellas block the sun's light so it can't warm those places as much.)

My science notebook: Read aloud the question on page 8: *How can you use shade to keep things cool?* Write the question on the board. Then have students draw in their science notebook a picture of a cool, shady place such as a shady spot next to a tree, shade under a canopy, or the shady side of a house. Help them write the word *shade* as a picture title and the word *cool* in the shady part of their picture.

- Explain that engineers are people who use science, math, and other knowledge to find solutions to problems. Say: **In this lesson, you will use your ideas about sun and shade to solve a problem.** Point to the question on the board; say: **How can you use shade to keep things cool?**
- Have students look at the steps on page 9. Say: **These are the steps you will use to solve the problem.** Read the steps aloud. Explain that each group will follow these steps and will record their observations in their science notebook. They will plan, build, and test a structure that uses shade to keep things cool. They will look at their results and consider whether they can improve on their plan. Then they will share their results with the class.
- Before students start working on their plans, show them the sunny spot where their structure is to be placed. Share any space constraints they must account for in their designs. Explain that they will leave their designs in the sun for one hour.

EXPLORE

Make a plan.

My science notebook Ask questions to help students form ideas, such as:

- **What will your structure look like?**
- **What part will make shade to keep things cool?**

Have students draw their ideas in their science notebook.

- Give students an opportunity to look at the materials available for building their structure. Ask questions to help students choose materials, such as:
  - **What materials do you need?**
  - **What will make your structure stand?**
  - **What material will make shade?**
  - **How will you know whether your structure works?**

Have students draw or list the materials they need in their science notebook.

SCIENCE AND ENGINEERING PRACTICES

Constructing Explanations and Designing Solutions

- In this activity, students use tools and/or materials to design and build a structure that provides shade to keep them cool. They test their structures and provide evidence about how well their structure solved a specific problem.

CROSSCUTTING CONCEPTS

Cause and Effect

- Say: **Engineers know that events have causes that generate observable patterns.** Ask: **What pattern did you notice when you were completing this activity?** (Possible answers: Some materials reduced the warming effect of sunlight better than others. Things I can see through didn't block much, or any of the light. Things under the structure stayed cooler. Things I couldn't see through blocked more sunlight and kept things under the structure cooler.)

Design a Structure (continued)

EXPLORE (continued)

Follow your plan.

- Remind students that their structure must use shade to keep things cool. They will need to work within the constraints of the available materials.
- If groups are struggling, ask questions to help them decide how to build their structure:
  - **What materials will you use for the bottom, the middle, and the top of your structure?**
  - **How will these you hold the parts of your structure together?**
  - **How will you make sure that you can move your structure to the place where you will test it?**

Test your structure.

- Take students to the testing site if it is in a place other than your classroom. Assist students in moving their structures as necessary.
- Help students place their structures in such a way that they do not cast shade on other groups' designs. Then have students observe and record the relative temperature of the area under their structure *and* the area that is not covered by the structure. They will need to compare these observations with their observations after the test in order to determine if their structure worked.
- After one hour, return to the testing site. Ask questions to guide students in making their observations.
  - **What did the area under your structure feel like before the test? After the test?**
  - **What did the area that was not shaded by your structure feel like before the test? After the test?**
- Have students draw or write the results of their test in their science notebook.

EXPLAIN

Revise your structure.

- Remind students to look at the pictures and words they recorded in their science notebook. Explain that these pictures and words are called *data*. Their data will help them decide whether their structure uses shade to keep things cool.
- Allow groups to reconvene to analyze their results. Ask questions to guide them, such as:
  - **What was the problem?**
  - **Did your structure solve the problem?**
  - **How could you change your structure to make it work better?**
- If time permits, have groups optimize their designs by revising and testing again. When groups are satisfied with their results, have each group prepare a summary that explains what they did and how it worked.
- Say: **Engineers use tools and materials provided to design and build a device that solves a specific problem or a solution to a specific problem.** Ask: **How did you think like an engineer as you completed this activity?** (I used materials in my classroom to make a structure that blocks sunlight.)

Share your results.

- Have each group share their plan and the structure they built with the class. Encourage students to use drawings and other data from their science notebook to support the design of their structure.
- Have each group tell how they tested the structure and how well the structure worked to solve the problem. If students were able to revise their designs, have them explain how the changes they made affected their results. Allow other students to ask questions and suggest improvements.

ELABORATE

- Extend the investigation by having students revise their plans based on feedback from the class. If possible, display the final structures.
- Have students use materials from home to build a different structure to solve the same problem. Allow time for students to present their plans, results, and conclusions to the class.

EVALUATE

Check to make sure that students have included drawings of their ideas, a list of the materials they used, and their test results in their science notebook. Then ask students these questions. Have them draw or write the answers in their science notebook.

1. **EXPLAIN How can you use shade to keep things cool?** (You can make a structure that blocks sunlight. Things that are under the structure will be in shade and will stay cooler than things that have the sun shining directly on them.)
2. **EVALUATE What kinds of materials would not be a good choice for building a structure to use shade to keep things cool?** (Materials that do not block sunlight, such as glass, clear plastic, and a material with holes in it, would not block the sun and would not make a shady place.)

RUBRICS

Teacher Rubric Use the scale descriptions to guide your assessment of the student's work. Assess each item separately, and then decide on one overall score, using the following scale:

4: Student performs with thorough understanding.
3: Student performs with adequate understanding.
2: Student performs with basic understanding.
1: Student performs with limited understanding.

Rubric	Scale			
The student made a plan to design a structure by drawing ideas and materials to solve a problem.	4	3	2	1
The student built a structure—based on his or her plan—to solve a problem and tested the structure.	4	3	2	1
The student determined whether that structure solved the problem. The student revised and retested the structure based on observations and feedback from others.	4	3	2	1
The student shared his/her final design, using evidence from his/her observations to support his/her conclusions.	4	3	2	1
Overall Score	4	3	2	1

Student Rubric Have students complete a self-evaluation similar to the one shown below.

Rubric	Yes	Not Yet
1 I can make a plan and choose materials to solve a problem.		
2 I can build a structure to solve a problem and test the structure.		
3 I can decide whether my structure solved the problem and change the structure if I need to.		
4 I can use the drawings I made in my science notebook to explain my results.		

The Weather

NEXT GENERATION SCIENCE STANDARDS | DISCIPLINARY CORE IDEAS

ESS2.D: Weather and Climate Weather is the combination of sunlight, wind, snow or rain, and temperature in a particular region at a particular time. (K-ESS2-1)

Objective Students will be able to:

- Recall that weather is what the air is like outside.

Science Vocabulary

weather, temperature

ENGAGE

Tap Prior Knowledge

- Ask students to recall words that describe different kinds of weather. Write their weather words on the board. (Possible words: *sunny, windy, raining, snowing, sleeting, hailing, freezing, cool, hot, warm*) Ask: **Which of these words describe today's weather?** (Answers should reflect the region where students live.)

EXPLORE

Preview the Lesson

- Read aloud the lesson's main heading. Say: **The main heading of this lesson is *The Weather.*** Draw a word web on the board. Write the word *weather* in the center oval of the web.
- Explain that the pictures on pages 10–11 show different weather in the same place at different times of the year. Have students look at the large background picture on pages 10–11. Ask: **What words describe the weather in this picture?** (Possible answers: snowy, cloudy, icy) Record students' words in outer ovals on the word web.
- Have students look at the smaller inset picture on page 11. Ask: **What words describe the weather in this picture?** (Possible answers: warm, cloudy, and sunny) Add these words to the web.

Set a Purpose and Read

- Tell students to listen to find out what weather is.
- Have students follow along as you read pages 10–11.

EXPLAIN

Define Weather

- After reading pages 10–11, ask: **What is weather?** (Weather is what the air is like outside.) Have students recall key details of the text by asking: **What details does the text tell you about the weather?** (Weather changes from region to region. Some regions are cold in winter and warm in summer. Temperature means how warm or cold the air is.) Explain that a *region* is a large area or place.
- Say: **Think about where we live.** Ask: **What is the weather like today?** (Answers should reflect the current weather outside the classroom.) **What was the weather like yesterday?** (Answers should reflect the prior day's weather.)
- Ask: **How does the weather today compare with the weather yesterday?** (Answers should reflect the weather yesterday and today.)
- Say: **The region, or place, shown in these pictures has cold, snowy weather in winter and warm, sunny weather in summer.** Ask: **What is the weather like in our region in winter?** (Answers should reflect the region where students live.) **What is the weather in our region like in summer?** (Answers should reflect the region where students live.)
- Ask: **How does weather from different regions compare? How is it the same? How is it different?** (Answers should reflect the weather in different regions.)

Describe Temperature

- Remind students of the two activities they have carried out in this unit. Point out that in both of these activities, students measured how warm or cool materials were. Write the word *temperature* on the board. Say: **The temperature is the measure of how warm or cold the air is.** Ask: **What is the temperature outside like today?** (Answers should reflect the day's relative temperature. Students should use words such as *cold, cool, hot,* or *warm.*) Point to the winter picture. Ask: **Do you think the temperature in this picture is warm or cold?** (cold) **How can you tell?** (I see snow on the ground and ice on the river.) Point to the summer picture. Ask: **Do you think the temperature in this picture is warm or cold?** (warm) **How can you tell?** (There is no snow.)

ELABORATE

Record Your Ideas About Weather

My science notebook Have students fold a sheet of white paper in half to make a four-page booklet. Have them title the booklet *Some Kinds of Weather.* Then have them draw pictures of different kinds of weather, such as sunny, rainy, windy, and snowy. As you continue through the lessons, have students add words to their booklets that correspond to the different kinds of weather.

Extend Your Thinking About Regional Weather

My science notebook Help students research weather in several regions around the country. This is most easily done using Internet sources or weather data in newspapers. Display a map of the United States and record the high temperature cities in five or six different regions. Discuss with students whether the temperatures displayed would be warm or cold.

EVALUATE

My science notebook Have students record the answer to the Wrap It Up question in their science notebook.

Wrap It Up!

1. **RECALL** **What is weather?** (Weather is what the air is like outside.)

SCIENCE MISCONCEPTIONS

Weather and Climate

People often use the terms *weather* and *climate* interchangeably. However, the terms actually represent two distinct concepts. Weather is the day-to-day conditions of Earth's atmosphere at a particular place and time. It includes temperature, humidity, precipitation, wind, air pressure, and other conditions. Climate, on the other hand, is the average weather conditions in one region over a long period of time, often 30 years. Climate zones on Earth include temperate, tropical, and polar. Many classifications systems describe climate variations in specific areas within these zones.

READING CONNECTION

Identify the Main Topic

With prompting and support, identify the main topic and retell key details of a text.

Guide students to identify the main topic and retell key details of the text. For example, in the EXPLORE section, point out the main heading before you read it aloud. Point out that these headings, can often identify or give clues to the main topic of a passage. After reading the heading, ask: **What does this heading tell you about the main topic?** In the EXPLAIN section when asking students to define weather, ask questions that help students understand that the answers they identify are the key details that support the main topic, for example: **What details does the text give you about the main topic? How is temperature related to weather?**

Sunny and Cloudy

NEXT GENERATION SCIENCE STANDARDS | DISCIPLINARY CORE IDEAS

ESS2.D: Weather and Climate Weather is the combination of sunlight, wind, snow or rain, and temperature in a particular region at a particular time. (K-ESS2-1)

Objective **Students will be able to:**
- Describe sunny weather and cloudy weather.

Science Vocabulary
cloudy, sunny

ENGAGE

Tap Prior Knowledge

- Have students observe the sky and describe what they see. If the day is sunny, remind students never to look directly at the sun. Say: **The sky does not always look this way.** Ask: **How else can the sky look during the day?** (Possible answers: The sun can shine in a clear, blue sky. The sky can have a few clouds, have many clouds, or be filled with clouds.)

EXPLORE

Preview the Lesson

- Read aloud the lesson's main heading. Ask: **What clues does the main heading give about the topic of this lesson?** (Possible answer: The lesson will be about sunny and cloudy weather.)
- Have students look at the large background picture on pages 12–13. Ask: **What kind of weather is shown in this picture?** (cloudy weather) **How do you know?** (The sky is full of dark clouds.)
- Have students look at the small inset picture on page 12. Ask: **What kind of weather is shown in this picture?** (sunny weather) **How do you know?** (The sky is blue, and it has no clouds.)

Set a Purpose and Read

- Have students follow along as you read in order to find out about sunny weather and cloudy weather.
- Read pages 12–13 aloud.

EXPLAIN

Describe Cloudy Weather and Sunny Weather

- After you read pages 12–13, write the word *cloudy* on the board. Ask: **What word do you see in the word *cloudy*?** (*cloud*) Underline the letters *c-l-o-u-d*. Say: ***Cloudy* means "full of clouds."** Ask: **How would you describe cloudy weather?** (Possible answers: The sky is full of clouds. You can't see the sun.)
- Write the word *sunny* on the board. Ask: **What word do you see in the word *sunny*?** (*sun*) Underline the letters *s-u-n*. Say: ***Sunny* means "full of sun."** Ask: **How would you describe sunny weather?** (Possible answers: The sky is blue. There are few or no clouds. You can see the sun.)
- Point out that the big picture on pages 12–13 shows the sky almost completely covered with clouds and the small picture on page 12 shows the sky with no clouds. Say: **When you look outside, sometimes the sky looks different from these two pictures. Sometimes the sky has a few clouds, but the weather is mostly sunny. Other times the sky has a lot of clouds, but you can still see the sun. At those times the weather is partly cloudy.**
- On the board, draw a horizontal line to represent the horizon. Then draw the sun in the sky. Say: **Here is a picture of the sky.** Ask: **Is the weather sunny or cloudy?** (sunny) **How can you tell?** (The sun is in the sky. There are no clouds.)

- Add a couple clouds to the picture. Ask: **What is the weather like now?** (It is still sunny.) **Explain.** (Even when there are a few clouds in the sky, the weather is sunny if you can see the sun and the sky is mostly blue.)
- Add more clouds until they cover the whole sky, including the sun. Ask: **What is the weather like now?** (It is cloudy.) **What happened to the sun?** (Clouds covered it.) Discuss how the sun does not disappear, or go away, when the weather is cloudy. Say: **Clouds can hide the sun, but the sun still is shining brightly.**

ELABORATE

Find Out More About Sunny Weather and Cloudy Weather

Have students apply their understanding of sunny weather and cloudy weather by painting one picture showing a sunny day and another picture showing a cloudy day. Ask: **What is the most important object to show on your sunny day picture?** (the sun) **What is the most important object to show on your cloudy day picture?** (clouds) Help students label their pictures, and display them in the classroom.

Extend Your Thinking About Sunny Weather and Cloudy Weather

Help students understand that the terms *sunny day* and *cloudy day* are relative. Project on a whiteboard or show a variety of pictures showing a range of sky images from totally cloudy to partly cloudy to mostly sunny to totally clear. Have volunteers tell whether each image is cloudy or sunny and explain why they made their choice.

EVALUATE

Have students record the answer to the Wrap It Up question in their science notebook.

Wrap It Up!

1. DESCRIBE **Describe a sunny day.** (You can see the sun on a sunny day. There are few or no clouds in the sky.)

SCIENCE MISCONCEPTIONS

Clouds and Rain

Some students may think that clouds are made of cotton, smoke, or steam. They may also think that rain comes from holes in clouds, much like salt comes out of a salt shaker.

In fact, clouds are made of tiny water droplets or ice crystals. The droplets or crystals fall to the ground when they become too heavy for the air to hold up. Typically, they fall as rain or snow.

READING CONNECTION

Describe Connections

With prompting and support, describe the connection between two individuals, events, ideas, or pieces of information in a text.

Guide students to describe the connection between two ideas in the text. For example, in the EXPLAIN section when asking students to describe sunny and cloudy weather, have them answer questions such as, **How are sunny weather and cloudy weather alike?** (Possible answers: Both are kinds of weather. Both describe how the sky looks.) **How are sunny weather and cloudy weather different?** (Possible answers: In sunny weather, the sky may have a few clouds, but it is mostly clear and blue, and you can see the sun. In cloudy weather, the sky is covered with white or gray clouds, and you can't see the sun.)

Windy Weather

NEXT GENERATION SCIENCE STANDARDS | DISCIPLINARY CORE IDEAS
ESS2.D: Weather and Climate Weather is the combination of sunlight, wind, snow or rain, and temperature in a particular region at a particular time. (K-ESS2-1)

Objective **Students will be able to:**
- Infer from visual evidence whether the wind is blowing.

Science Vocabulary
wind

ENGAGE

Tap Prior Knowledge

- Have students describe the wind in their own words. Then have them imagine they are standing in a strong wind. Ask: **What does the wind feel like? What do you see blowing in the strong wind?** (Possible answers: I can feel it blowing my hair and my clothes. I can feel it blowing on my face. I can see tree branches bending. I can see loose objects blowing away.)

EXPLORE

Preview the Lesson

- Read aloud the main heading. Ask: **What clues does the main heading give about the topic of this lesson?** (Possible answer: The lesson will be about windy weather.)
- Have students look at the small inset picture on page 14. Read aloud the caption. Ask: **What is the wind like in this picture? How do you know?** (There is no wind. I know because the flag is not moving.)
- Have students look at the large background picture on pages 14–15. Ask: **What is the wind like in this picture? How do you know?** (The wind is strong. The flag is flapping in the wind.)

Set a Purpose and Read

- Tell students to listen in order to find out about windy weather.
- Have students follow along as you read aloud pages 14–15.

EXPLAIN

Describe Windy Weather

- After you read pages 14–15, write the word *wind* on the board. Ask: **What is wind?** (moving air) Have students ask and answer questions about key details in the text, such as:
  - **Which sentence tells you what wind is?**
  - **Which words tell you how strongly wind can blow?**
  - **Which words tell you how you know that the wind is blowing?**
- Have students model the wind by blowing air on their hands, first gently, then strongly. Explain that you can feel the moving air from your mouth, just as you can feel the air outside on windy days. Say: **Wind can be gentle or strong.**

My science notebook Help students construct a chart in their science notebook, or construct a class chart, for recording observations about the wind. Remind students to use words or drawings or both to record data.

Example:

Day	Time	Wind
Monday	morning	gentle wind
Monday	lunch time	gentle wind
Monday	afternoon	strong wind
Tuesday	morning	no wind

- Have students observe the strength of the wind three times a day. Have them observe the same object, such as a flag or the branches of a tree, each time. Then have them describe the wind and record their descriptions in the chart.

- After a few days, review the entries with the class. Ask: **When was the wind the strongest? When was the wind very gentle?** (Answers should reflect the data on the chart.)
- Ask: **What does the chart show about the wind?** (Possible answers: The wind changes often. It can be different at different times on the same day. It can be gentle or strong. There can be no wind at all.)

ELABORATE

Find Out More About Wind

My science notebook

Have students wear safety goggles. Help students build simple pinwheels from construction paper, a thumbtack, and a pencil. Take students outside at different times of day and on different days to use their pinwheel to see variations in wind speed. Have students draw a picture of their pinwheel when the wind is gentle and when the wind is strong. Help students label their picture, using the words *gentle* and *strong*.

Extend Your Thinking About Wind

My science notebook

Help students make wind chimes to hear the sound of the wind and to compare the sound from a gentle wind to the sound from a strong wind. Suggestions for making wind chimes using simple materials, such as paper cups, paint, paintbrushes, metal washers, pipe cleaners, string, colorful beads, and small bells, can be found on the Internet. Help students hang their finished wind chimes in a place that is exposed to the wind so they can hear the sounds.

EVALUATE

My science notebook

Have students record the answer to the Wrap It Up question in their science notebook.

Wrap It Up!

1. INFER **What can you see in the picture that tells you the wind is blowing?** (I see the flag blowing in the wind.)

PHYSICAL SCIENCE
Forces and Interactions: Pushes and Pulls

LIFE SCIENCE
Interdependent Relationships in Ecosystems: Animals, Plants, and Their Environment

EARTH SCIENCE
Weather and Climate

SCIENCE BACKGROUND

Anemometer

An anemometer is an instrument that is used to measure wind speed. Anemometers are commonly used in weather stations. A widely-used type of anemometers is the cup anemometer. It has cups attached to the ends of horizontal arms. The arms are mounted at equal angles to each other on a vertical shaft. The cups catch the wind. This causes them to rotate. This turns the shaft. How many times it spins in a certain time period can give information about the wind speed.

READING CONNECTION

Retell Key Details

With prompting and support, ask and answer questions about key details in a text.

Guide students to ask and answer questions as they read to help them identify and understand key details in the text. For example, in the ENGAGE section before you set a purpose for reading, point out and read the main heading. Challenge students to look at the pictures and the heading and think of questions they have about windy weather. Have students listen for the answers to their questions as you read. Then in the EXPLAIN section have students discuss how the details in the text helped them answer their questions.

Wet Weather

NEXT GENERATION SCIENCE STANDARDS | DISCIPLINARY CORE IDEAS

ESS2.D: Weather and Climate Weather is the combination of sunlight, wind, snow or rain, and temperature in a particular region at a particular time. People measure these conditions to describe and record the weather and to notice patterns over time. (K-ESS2-1)

Objective Students will be able to:

- Describe rainy or snowy weather.

ENGAGE

Tap Prior Knowledge

- Have students describe a recent rainy or snowy day. Encourage them to include details, such as how long the rain or snow fell, what it sounded like, and how the rain or snow changed the outdoors.

EXPLORE

Preview the Lesson

- Read aloud the main heading. Then have students look at the small inset picture on page 16. Ask: **What do you see in this picture?** (Possible answer: I see rain falling on trees.) Read aloud the caption. Ask: **How often does rain fall where we live?** (Answers will vary. Possible answers: It hardly ever rains here. It often rains here in the winter, but not in the summer. Answers should reflect your local region.)
- Have students look at the large background picture on pages 16–17. Ask: **What do you see in this picture?** (Possible answer: I see snow falling on trees.) Read aloud the caption. Ask: **When does snow fall in our region?** (Answers will vary. Possible answers: It snows here in the winter. It never snows here. Answers should reflect the local region.)

Set a Purpose and Read

- Have students listen in order to find out about wet weather.
- Have students follow along as you read aloud pages 16–17.

EXPLAIN

Describe Rainy and Snowy Weather

- After you read pages 16–17, draw a word web on the board. Write *wet weather* in the center oval. Ask: **What details does the text tell you about wet weather?** (Sometimes clouds bring wet weather. Rain or snow falls from the clouds.)
- Ask: **What kind of wet weather does the small picture show?** (rain) Write the word *rain* in another oval in the web. Ask: **Where does rain come from?** (Rain falls from the clouds.) **What words can you use to describe rain?** (Possible answers: *wet, water, pouring, drizzling, makes puddles*) Add students' words to the web.
- Ask: **What kind of wet weather does the large picture show?** (snow) Write *snow* in another oval in the word web. Ask: **Where does snow come from?** (Snow falls from the clouds.) **What words can you use to describe snow?** (Possible answers: *wet, white, cold, covers the ground, piles up*) Add students' words to the web.

Measuring Rain and Snow

- Read aloud the first sentence on page 17. Say: **People can measure how much rain or snow falls.** Write the word *measure* on the board. Say: **In this lesson, *measure* means "to find out how much rain or snow fell in your region at a particular time.** Ask: **How could you measure how much rain falls?"** (Possible answer: I could put a measuring cup outside to catch the rain.) **How could you measure how much snow falls?** (Possible answer: I could take a ruler outside and stick it into the snow to see how deep it is.)

Understanding Patterns of Wet Weather

- Read aloud the second sentence on page 17. Say: **People can notice patterns of weather.** Write the word *pattern* on the board. Say: **A pattern is something that happens again and again. For example, the sun appearing to rise every morning is a pattern.**

- Say: **Snowfall in winter is a weather pattern in some places. If you live in those places, you expect snow in winter because snow in winter is a weather pattern.** Ask: **What is a weather pattern where we live?** (Answers will vary. Possible answer: It rains mostly in the winter here. It rains here, but it almost never snows.) Ask: **How do you think weather patterns can help people?** (Answers will vary. Possible answer: People know they need a warm coat in winter because the weather pattern is cold. Answers should reflect the region where students live.)

ELABORATE

Find Out More About Wet Weather

My science notebook Help students understand that different regions have different kinds of wet weather. Display pictures of a desert, including dry, cracked land; land with sagebrush and cactus; and sand dunes. Ask: **What do you think the wet weather pattern is in these deserts?** (Possible answer: It looks very dry, so it probably doesn't get very much rain.) Show pictures of Washington State including lush vegetation and rain and snow. Ask: **What do you think the wet weather pattern is in this region?** (Possible answer: It probably rains and snows a lot.)

Extend Your Thinking About Wet Weather

My science notebook Help students explore other kinds of wet weather, such as sleet and hail. Show pictures of sleet, and ask students to describe sleet. Then have students add the word *sleet* and their descriptive words to the wet weather word web. Display pictures of large hailstones, and ask students to describe hail. Then have students add the word *hail* and their descriptive words to the web. Ask students to compare and contrast the kinds of wet weather—rain, snow, sleet, and hail—on their word web.

EVALUATE

My science notebook Have students record the answer to the Wrap It Up question in their science notebook.

Wrap It Up!

1. **DESCRIBE** **What do you see on a rainy day?** (Answers will vary. Possible answers: I see rain falling from clouds. I see puddles on the ground. I see raindrops splashing on a car window. I see clouds in the sky.)

DIFFERENTIATED INSTRUCTION

Extra Support Have students draw two simple pictures of wet weather. One picture should show rain falling and the other picture should show snow falling. Help students label the appropriate picture *rain* or *snow*.

Challenge Ask students to recall how they might measure rain or snow. Then have them draw a picture of themselves measuring rain, perhaps using a measuring cup, or snow, perhaps using a ruler.

READING CONNECTION

Identify the Main Topic

With prompting and support, identify the main topic and retell key details of a text.

Guide students to identify the main topic and retell key details of the text. For example, in the EXPLORE section after you read the main heading, ask students to recall what clues this heading can give them. (It can give clues about the main topic of the lesson.) Then read the title aloud: *Wet Weather*. Point out that both pictures show types of wet weather. In the EXPLAIN section after reading the text aloud, ask questions that encourage students to retell key details. For example: **What falls from clouds?** (rain or snow) **What are two types of wet weather?** (rain and snow)

Investigate

Weather

NEXT GENERATION SCIENCE STANDARDS | PERFORMANCE EXPECTATION

K-ESS2-1. Use and share observations of local weather conditions to describe patterns over time. [Clarification Statement: Examples of qualitative observations could include descriptions of the weather (such as sunny, cloudy, rainy, and warm); examples of quantitative observations could include numbers of sunny, windy, and rainy days in a month. Examples of patterns could include that it is usually cooler in the morning than in the afternoon and the number of sunny days versus cloudy days in different months.] [*Assessment Boundary: Assessment of quantitative observations limited to whole numbers and relative measures such as warmer/cooler.*]

Objective **Students will be able to:**

- Observe local weather conditions to describe patterns over time.

CLASSROOM MANAGEMENT

Materials ***For groups of 4:*** weather chart; pencil or crayons

Time 20 minutes in the morning each day for a week; 20 minutes in the afternoon each day for a week

Advance Preparation Make a weather chart for students to record their observations. The chart might be a class chart on chart paper or the whiteboard, or you may wish to make each student a copy of the blackline master *Weather*, provided in both English and Spanish on pages E39–E40 of this Teacher Guide.

Teaching Tips Be sure students understand the meaning of the words and symbols on the chart. Have students stand in the same place in the morning and afternoon each day for a more accurate comparison. After all observations are complete, challenge students to find a pattern in the weather for the week. For example, the weather may have been cool enough that you needed a jacket every day, or the weather may have been such that you needed a jacket in the morning but not in the afternoon.

What to Expect Students will observe the weather in the morning and in the afternoon each day for a week. They will observe in order to answer the question, *Do you need a jacket?* Students will observe temperature, cloud cover, wind, and rain to make their decisions. Students will record each observation on the weather chart by circling or coloring either the jacket symbol or the T-shirt symbol. After all observations are complete, students will compare and contrast the morning and afternoon weather each day and throughout the week to identify patterns.

ENGAGE

Tap Prior Knowledge

- Ask: **What kinds of weather have we learned about?** (Possible answers: sunny, cloudy, windy, wet, warm, cold). Have volunteers describe each kind of weather.
- Ask: **Which of these weather conditions help you decide what clothes, jackets, shoes, and hats to wear?** (Answers will vary. Possible answer: All of these weather conditions affect what you wear.)

EXPLORE

- Guide students through the investigation. Read pages 18–19 together.

  My science notebook — Have students use or make a weather chart for recording their observations in their science notebook.
- Before students do steps 1 and 2, write the word *observe* on the board. Ask: **What do you do when you observe something?** (Possible answer: You look carefully at something and use your senses to learn about it.)
- Then write the word *record* on the board. Ask: **What do you do when you record something?** (Possible answer: You draw or write down your observations.)

- Explain the weather chart to students by reading the words aloud and modeling how to record each observation by circling or coloring either the jacket or the T-shirt.
- Ask: **How will you decide whether you need a jacket?** (Possible answers: I will feel how warm or cold it is outside. If it's raining, I might decide that I need a jacket to stay dry even if it is warm.)

EXPLAIN

- Have students share their observations with the class. Pose questions to help students discover any patterns. For example, ask:
  - **What was the weather like when you needed a jacket?** (Possible answers: It was cool/cold. It was windy. It was cloudy. It was raining/snowing.)
  - **What was the weather like when you did NOT need a jacket?** (Possible answers: It was sunny. It was warm. The wind was blowing gently. It was cloudy and warm. It was not raining.)
- Ask: **Did you see any patterns in when you needed a jacket and when you did not? Explain.** (Answers will vary, based on the data on students' charts. Students may find that they needed a jacket more often in the morning than in the afternoon. Explanations could include that sunlight warms the air during the day, so it is warmer in the afternoon than in the morning.)

ELABORATE

- Have students continue their observations over the course of a month. Remind them to record their observations. Ask them to identify any patterns they notice. For example, if this activity is carried out in the spring, students may notice that they need a jacket on fewer and fewer days as the weather warms. The opposite could be true if this activity is carried out in the fall.

EVALUATE

My science notebook

Have students record the answers to the Wrap It Up questions in their science notebook.

Wrap It Up!

1. CONTRAST **How was the morning weather different from the afternoon?** (Answers will vary depending on weather conditions observed. Possible answer: The morning weather was cooler than the afternoon weather.)
2. COMPARE **How were they the same?** (Answers will vary depending on weather conditions observed. Possible answer: The weather was cool in both morning and afternoon, or raining in the morning and not in the afternoon.)

SCIENCE AND ENGINEERING PRACTICES

Analyzing and Interpreting Data

- In this activity, students observe and record their observations about the weather pattern they observe from morning to afternoon. Ask students to give examples of how they can use the data they collected. (Possible answers: I can observe how the weather changes and can plan what kind of coat I will need when I go outside.)

Connections to Nature of Science
Science Knowledge is Based on Empirical Evidence

- Point out to students that scientists look for patterns and order when making observations about the world. Ask: **Did you notice any patterns in the weather that we observed that might lead you to predict what the weather will be like tomorrow?** (Answers can vary depending on the season, but students may respond that the weather might follow a similar pattern.)

Weather Patterns

NEXT GENERATION SCIENCE STANDARDS | DISCIPLINARY CORE IDEAS

ESS2.D: Weather and Climate Weather is the combination of sunlight, wind, snow or rain, and temperature in a particular region at a particular time. People measure these conditions to describe and record the weather and to notice patterns over time. (K-ESS2-1)

Objective Students will be able to:
- Describe weather patterns.

ENGAGE

Tap Prior Knowledge

- Have students recall the *Investigate* about weather. Ask: **What weather patterns did you observe during that *Investigate*?** (Possible answers: Morning weather was often different from afternoon weather. Morning was usually cool, and afternoon was usually warmer.)
- Ask: **What other weather patterns have you seen?** (Possible answers: I saw rain change to snow. I saw a calm day change to a windy day. I noticed that during one week each day was warmer than the day before.)

EXPLORE

Preview the Lesson

- Read and discuss the main heading of the lesson. Then have students observe the large background picture on pages 20–21. Ask: **What weather does this picture show?** (Possible answers: It shows a sunny day with just a few clouds in the sky.) **How can you tell that the sun is shining?** (Possible answers: I see the shadow of the big tower in the pool of water. I see sunlight shining on the gold dome in the background. Everything in the picture looks bright.)
- Have students look at the small inset picture on page 21. Ask: **What weather does this picture show?** (Possible answers: It shows a rainy day with clouds covering the sky. The top of the big tower is covered with clouds.) **How can you tell that it's raining?** (Possible answer: The person in the picture is holding an open umbrella.)

Set a Purpose and Read

- Tell students to listen to find out about weather patterns.
- Have students follow along as you read pages 20–21.

EXPLAIN

Identify Weather Patterns Over Time

- After reading pages 20–21, help students identify key details about weather patterns in the text. Read aloud the first sentence on page 20. Ask: **What does that sentence tell you about weather patterns?** (Possible answer: Weather is not the same all the time. It changes.)
- Read aloud the second sentence on page 20. Ask: **What does that sentence tell you about weather patterns?** (Possible answer: Weather can be different from one day to the next.) Say: **Give me an example a time of when you experienced the weather changing from one day to the next.** (Possible answers: I remember last week when Monday was sunny and Tuesday was rainy. I remember when it was very cold one day and then much warmer the next day.)
- Read aloud the first sentence on page 21. Ask: **What does that sentence tell you about weather patterns?** (Possible answer: Weather can change during a day.) Say: **Tell me about a time you experienced a change in the weather during one day.** (Sample answer: One day started out sunny and warm. Then it got windy and clouds covered the sky. By nighttime it was raining.)

ELABORATE

Find Out More About Weather Patterns

My science notebook Help students identify weather patterns in your region throughout the year. Using various colors of cardstock, write each month of the year on a separate 8½" x 11" sheet. To help students connect to each month, ask them to name special things that happen in each month every year. Record their ideas on the cards. For example, you might record the beginning of summer, the start of school, the end of the calendar year, the seasons, and even students' birthdays. Then ask: **What weather patterns do you recall in January in this region?** (Answers will depend on your local weather.) Ask questions and record students' answers for each month. Display the cards, and have students compare weather patterns in your region at different times of the year.

Extend Your Thinking About Weather Patterns

My science notebook Help students understand that weather patterns are different in different places on Earth. Ask: **What weather patterns do you recall in summer in this region? What weather patterns do you recall in winter in this region?** (Answers will vary with location.) Help students research average temperatures in regions with very different weather patterns, such as Alaska and the Caribbean. You may wish to use simple bar graphs to show how the temperatures in these two regions differ throughout the year. Help students compare weather patterns in these regions with weather patterns in your region.

EVALUATE

My science notebook Have students record the answer to the Wrap It Up question in their science notebook.

Wrap It Up!

1. CONTRAST **How is the rainy day different from the sunny day?** (On the rainy day the sky is covered with clouds. Rain is falling from the clouds. You can't see the sun. On the sunny day the sky is mostly a clear blue with just a few clouds. The sun is shining.)

ELL SUPPORT

Identify Weather Patterns

Beginning Ask yes/no questions, such as: **Does weather change from day to day?** (Yes.) **Is the weather always the same in morning and afternoon?** (No.)

Intermediate Provide sentence frames, such as: *Weather can (change) from day to day. Weather can be cool in the (morning) and warm in the (afternoon).*

Advanced Help students complete sentence stems about weather patterns. Provide these stems: *Weather changes … Weather can be sunny in the morning and …*

READING CONNECTION

Identify the Main Topic

With prompting and support, identify the main topic and retell key details of a text.

Guide students to identify the main topic and retell key details of the text. For example, in the EXPLORE section, discuss the main heading and have students explain what clues this heading gives them about the main topic of the lesson. In the EXPLAIN section, use the series of questions on page 20 to guide students in retelling the key details in the text in their own words.

Investigate

Weather Patterns

NEXT GENERATION SCIENCE STANDARDS | PERFORMANCE EXPECTATION

K-ESS2-1. Use and share observations of local weather conditions to describe patterns over time. [Clarification Statement: Examples of qualitative observations could include descriptions of the weather (such as sunny, cloudy, rainy, and warm); examples of quantitative observations could include numbers of sunny, windy, and rainy days in a month. Examples of patterns could include that it is usually cooler in the morning than in the afternoon and the number of sunny days versus cloudy days in different months.] [*Assessment Boundary: Assessment of quantitative observations limited to whole numbers and relative measures such as warmer/cooler.*]

Objective Students will be able to:

- Observe local weather conditions to describe patterns over time.

CLASSROOM MANAGEMENT

Materials ***For groups of 4:*** weather patterns chart; pencil or crayons

Time 20 minutes on Monday; 10 minutes each day, Tuesday–Thursday; 15 minutes on Friday

Advance Preparation Make a weather patterns chart for students to record their observations. The chart might be a class chart on chart paper or the whiteboard, or you may wish to make a copy for each student of the blackline master *Weather Patterns*, provided in both English and Spanish on pages E41–E42 of this Teacher Guide.

Teaching Tips Be sure students understand the meanings of the words and symbols on the chart. You may wish to display a list of words for students to record on the weather patterns chart, based on their suggestions, such as *cold* or *warm* for the *Temperature* column; *cloudy* or *sunny* for the *Clouds* column; *strong* or *gentle* for the *Wind* column; and *rainy, snowy,* or *clear* for the *Rain* column.

What to Expect Students will observe the average daily weather each day for a week in order to answer the question, *How does weather change from day to day?* Their observations will include temperature, cloud cover, wind, and rain. They will record their observations on a weather patterns chart. After all observations are complete, students will describe local weather patterns over time, citing evidence from their weather patterns chart.

ENGAGE

Tap Prior Knowledge

- Write the words *temperature, clouds, wind,* and *rain* on the board. As you ask these questions, write students' ideas in a column under the appropriate weather word. Ask:
  - **What words do you know that describe the temperature outside?** (*cold, hot, cool, warm*)
  - **What words do you know that describe how the sky looks?** (*cloudy, sunny*)
  - **What words do you know that describe wind?** (*windy, calm, gentle, strong*)
  - **What words do you know that describe rain?** (*rainy, pouring, stormy, drizzling*)

EXPLORE

- Guide students through the investigation. Read pages 22–23 together.

  My science notebook Have students use or make a weather patterns chart for recording their observations in their science notebook.
- Before students carry out steps 1–2, review the meanings of the words *observe* and *record*. (*Observe* means "to look carefully at something and use your senses to learn about it." *Record* means "to draw or write down your observations.") Extend this idea by asking, **How are observing and recording connected?** Guide students to understand that by accurately recording their observations, they will be better able to identify weather patterns that may exist.
- Explain the weather chart to students by reading the words aloud and modeling how to record each observation by writing a word that describes the weather in each column across the page. Point to the list of weather words on the

board, and remind students that they can use that list to choose the appropriate words.

- Pose questions to help students with their observations. For example, ask: **If the weather is rainy most of the day and then gets sunny, what will you record?** (Possible answers: mostly rainy; rainy and sunny)

EXPLAIN

- Have students share their observations with the class. Pose questions to help students discover any patterns. For example, ask:
  - **Did any days have exactly the same weather all day long?**
  - **Were all days nearly the same temperature, or were one or two days much warmer or colder than the other days?**
- Have students cite evidence from their charts to support the patterns they describe. (Answers will vary based on the data on students' charts.)

ELABORATE

- Have students explore how weather affects what they do and what they wear. Help students make a chart. Each day for a week, have students record data in their science notebook to show how weather affected them.

Example:

Day of the Week	Weather	What I Did	What I Wore
Monday	cold, snowy	sledding	boots, winter coat, warm hat

After five days, have students share with the class how weather affected them. Remind students to cite evidence to support their conclusions. Encourage students to use the data in their charts.

EVALUATE

My science notebook

Have students record their answers to the Wrap It Up questions in their science notebook.

Wrap It Up!

1. DESCRIBE **How many days were sunny?** (Answers will vary, depending on weather conditions observed. Students may say that a certain number of days were sunny and then changed to cloudy.)
2. DESCRIBE **How many days were sunny? How many days were cloudy?** (Answers will vary, depending on weather conditions observed. Students may say that a certain number of days were cloudy and then changed to sunny.)

SCIENCE AND ENGINEERING PRACTICES

Analyzing and Interpreting Data

- In this activity students used observations to describe patterns in the local weather over time. Have students research the weather in another part of the country and describe the patterns in that location based on the data they observe.

Connections to Nature of Science
Science Knowledge is Based on Empirical Evidence

- Discuss with students that scientists look for patterns and order when making observations about the world. Tell them that they are thinking like scientists when they make observations and then make predictions based on their observations.

CROSSCUTTING CONCEPTS

Patterns

- Scientists know that patterns in the natural world can be observed, used to describe phenomena, and used as evidence.
- Remind students that they have been looking at weather patterns. Ask if they can think of any other patterns from their science studies. Students may mention patterns in leaves or flowers.

Thunderstorms and Tornadoes

NEXT GENERATION SCIENCE STANDARDS | DISCIPLINARY CORE IDEAS
ESS3.B: Natural Hazards Some kinds of severe weather are more likely than others in a given region. (K-ESS3-2)

Objective **Students will be able to:**

- Describe and compare two kinds of severe weather—thunderstorms and tornadoes.

Science Vocabulary
thunderstorm, tornado

ENGAGE

Tap Prior Knowledge

- Have students recall their experiences with a very bad storm. Say: **Describe what you saw, felt, and heard during a bad storm.** (Possible answers: Wind was blowing so hard it almost knocked me down. Huge raindrops were falling fast. Lightning flashed in the sky. I heard loud rumbles of thunder.)

EXPLORE

Preview the Lesson

- Have students observe the large background picture on pages 24–25. Ask: **What weather does this picture show?** (Possible answers: It shows lightning in the sky. It might be a thunderstorm.)
- Say: **Look at the lines of lightning in the sky. Those lines are called *lightning strokes*.** Ask: **How are the lightning strokes in this picture alike and different?** (Possible answers: *Alike:* They're all wiggly. They're all in the sky. *Different:* Some lightning strokes are thicker than others. Some stay in the sky, but others go down and touch the ground.)
- Have students look at the small inset picture on page 25. Ask: **What weather does this picture show?** (Possible answers: It shows a long tube coming down from the clouds. It shows a tornado.)

Set a Purpose and Read

- Tell students to listen to find out about thunderstorms and tornadoes.
- Have students follow along as you read pages 24–25.

EXPLAIN

Describe Thunderstorms and Tornadoes

- After reading pages 24–25, help students determine the meaning of *thunderstorm*. Write *thunderstorm* on the board. Ask: **What two words do you see in the word *thunderstorm*?** (I see the words *thunder* and *storm*.) **What is thunder?** (Thunder is a very loud sound.) **What is a storm?** (A storm is bad weather. It might have rain or snow and wind.) Read aloud the sentence on page 24 that defines thunderstorm: *A thunderstorm has rain, thunder, and lightning.* Point out to students that thunderstorms can occur almost everywhere. In the United States, Florida has more thunderstorms than any other state. Alabama, Louisiana, New Mexico, and Texas also have a lot of thunderstorms.
- Help students understand that both thunderstorms and tornadoes are dangerous. Ask: **Why do you think it might be dangerous to be near a window during a thunderstorm?** (Possible answers: Lightning might strike near the window. Strong winds might blow objects at a window and break it. If you are standing near the window, you might get hurt.)
- Point to the tornado on page 25. Have a volunteer find the term *tornado* in the text. Ask: **What does the text say that a tornado is?** (a wind that spins very fast) **Describe the tornado in the picture?** (It is the thing that looks like a tube.) Explain that the tube is the fast-spinning wind. Tornadoes can be thin or very wide. They can state on the ground over 80.4 kilometers (50 miles) Tornadoes may be hard to see until they pick up dust and debris or until a cloud forms over the funnel.
- Ask: **Why do you think a tornado might be dangerous?** (Possible answers: A tornado has winds that spin very fast. The winds carry

dirt and other things with them. The strong spinning winds could knock down buildings or trees.)

Compare and Contrast Thunderstorms and Tornadoes

- Draw a Venn diagram on the board. Write the word *thunderstorm* in the left oval, the word *tornado* in the right oval, and the word *both* in the space where the ovals overlap. Help students compare and contrast thunderstorms and tornadoes by asking questions, such as: **What is a thunderstorm like? What is a tornado like? How are these two kinds of weather alike? How are they different?** Write students' ideas in the appropriate parts of the Venn diagram.

ELABORATE

Model the Spinning of a Tornado

Help students model a tornado vortex using a 1-liter plastic bottle, water, and a basin to catch the water. You can find a video of this activity by searching the Internet for "tornado in a bottle." Students can vary this activity to make the vortex more visible. For example, they can add colored lamp oil or fine glitter to the water before modeling the vortex.

Extend Your Thinking About Safety During Severe Weather

Help students find out what kinds of severe weather are common in your region. Help students use the Internet to research safety tips for tornadoes, thunderstorms, and floods. Have students draw pictures of tips about how to stay safe during specific kinds of severe weather. Label students' drawings and display them in the classroom. You may wish to have students share the safety tips with other classes.

EVALUATE

Have students record the answer to the Wrap It Up question in their science notebook.

Wrap It Up!

1. **COMPARE How are tornadoes and thunderstorms alike?** (Both are dangerous. Both can have strong winds.)

SCIENCE BACKGROUND

Tornadoes

A tornado is a violently rotating column of air. About 69 percent of all tornadoes are "weak" tornadoes that have wind speeds of less than 177 kilometers per hour (110 mph) and last 1–10 minutes. About 29 percent are "strong" tornadoes that have wind speeds of 177–330 kilometers per hour (110–205 mph) and last about 20 minutes. About 2 percent are "violent" tornadoes that have wind speeds of up to 480 kilometers per hour (300 mph) and can last an hour or longer. The United States has the most tornadoes of any region on Earth, about 1,000 every year. Many of these tornadoes occur in an area of the Midwest called *Tornado Alley*, which includes the states of Texas, Oklahoma, Kansas, Nebraska, and Iowa.

READING CONNECTION

Understand Unknown Words

With prompting and support, ask and answer questions about unknown words in a text.

Guide students to ask and answer questions about unknown words in the text. As you set a purpose for reading in the EXPLORE section, point out the bold words *thunderstorm* and *tornado*. Explain that the bold black type indicates that these are important words to know. Also point out that these same words appear in the main heading. Guide students in crafting questions about these terms that could be answered using context clues. For example, **What is a thunderstorm? What is a tornado? What should I know about these storms?** Encourage students to find the answers to these questions as they read.

Blizzards and Hurricanes

NEXT GENERATION SCIENCE STANDARDS | DISCIPLINARY CORE IDEAS
ESS3.B: Natural Hazards Some kinds of severe weather are more likely than others in a given region. (K-ESS3-2)

Objective **Students will be able to:**
- Describe and compare two kinds of severe weather—blizzards and hurricanes.

Science Vocabulary
blizzard, hurricane

ENGAGE

Tap Prior Knowledge

- Have students recall what they learned about thunderstorms and tornadoes from the previous lesson. Ask: **How are thunderstorms and tornadoes alike?** (Both are dangerous. Both can have wind.) **How are they different?** (A tornado is a spinning wind that is part of a bigger storm. A thunderstorm is a storm with rain, thunder, and lightning and sometimes strong winds.)

EXPLORE

Preview the Lesson

- Have students observe the large background picture on pages 26–27. Ask: **What weather does this picture show?** (Possible answers: It shows a snowstorm. It shows a winter storm.)
- Have students look at the small inset picture on page 27. Ask: **What does this picture show?** (Possible answer: It shows a big wave.)

Set a Purpose and Read

- Tell students to listen to find out about blizzards and hurricanes.
- Have students follow along as you read pages 26–27.

EXPLAIN

Describe Thunderstorms and Tornadoes

- After reading pages 26–27, write *blizzard* on the board. Point out the sentences on page 26 that define and describe a blizzard. Have students examine the large picture of the blizzard. Ask: **What words would you use to describe this blizzard?** (Possible answers: snowy, white, hard to see, snow covers everything.) **What would the temperature feel like?** (Possible answer: It would feel cold.) **What do you think you would hear?** (Possible answer: I might hear the wind blowing. It might be very quiet. I would hear the truck plowing the snow.) Read aloud the caption on page 26. Ask: **Why do you think it is hard to see during a blizzard?** (Possible answers: There's so much snow coming down and blowing around. It's hard to see through so much snow.)
- Write *hurricane* on the board. Point out the sentences on page 27 that define and describe a hurricane. Have students look at the inset picture on page 27. Read aloud the caption. Ask: **What is flooding?** (Possible answers: Flooding is lots of water covering land that is usually dry. It's when everything is underwater.) **What two ways is water coming onto the land in this picture?** (Rain is coming from the clouds in the sky, and big waves are coming in from the ocean.)

Compare and Contrast Blizzards and Hurricanes

- Help students understand that both blizzards and hurricanes are dangerous. Ask: **Why do you think blizzards are dangerous?** (Possible answers: If you can't see in a blizzard, you might bump into things. People driving a car might crash. When it snows, surfaces get slippery, so people might fall or cars might slide. The strong winds and cold temperatures might make a person freeze.)
- Ask: **Why do you think a hurricane might be dangerous?** (Possible answers: The strong winds might knock over trees, and the trees might hit buildings. The winds might blow around furniture and trash cans that are outside. These objects could break windows. Flood waters might cover the road and make it impossible to drive away.)
- Draw a Venn diagram on the board. Write the word *blizzard* in the left oval, the word *hurricane* in the right oval, and the word *both* in the space where the ovals overlap. Help students compare

and contrast blizzards and hurricanes by asking questions, such as: **What is a blizzard like? What is a hurricane like? How are these two kinds of storms alike? How are they different?** Write students' ideas in the appropriate parts of the Venn diagram.

ELABORATE

Find Out More About Severe Weather

My science notebook

Have students share their personal experiences with severe weather by having them dictate anecdotes. Write each anecdote on the bottom half of a sheet of paper. Then have students draw a picture above their anecdote to illustrate it. Display the pictures and stories in the classroom.

Extend Your Thinking About Severe Weather

My science notebook

Explain that weather scientists at the World Meteorological Organization give each hurricane a name. Hurricanes are named so scientists can distinguish one from the others. The first storm every year gets a name that begins with the letter *A*. The second storm name begins with the letter *B*. The names continue alphabetically from A to W, but they skip *Q*, U, X, Y, and Z. The names alternate between male and female. There are six lists of names that are used over and over again. If a hurricane is very destructive, its name is taken off the list and replaced with another name starting with the same letter. The six lists of hurricane names for the Atlantic Ocean can be found on the Internet. Search for "hurricane names."

EVALUATE

My science notebook

Have students record the answer to the Wrap It Up question in their science notebook.

Wrap It Up!

1. COMPARE **How are blizzards and hurricanes alike?** (Both are dangerous storms. Both have strong winds. Both involve wet [rainy or snowy] weather.)

TEACHING WITH TECHNOLOGY

Blizzards and Hurricanes

Project on a whiteboard pictures from the Internet of blizzards in progress. Show whiteout conditions during the storm in several settings. Ask volunteers to circle evidence of strong winds, a lot of snow, and a lack of visibility. Also show the aftermath of blizzards. Ask volunteers to circle evidence of the blizzard, such as large amounts of snow, cars buried in snow, and fallen utility poles and wires.

Next, project pictures of hurricanes. Show the circular formation and the eye of the hurricane in a satellite view. Show a hurricane in progress. Ask volunteers to circle evidence of strong winds, heavy rain, and huge waves in the ocean. Also show the destruction caused by hurricanes. Ask volunteers to circle evidence of the hurricane, such as fallen trees, destroyed buildings, and damaged bridges.

READING CONNECTION

Understand Unknown Words

With prompting and support, ask and answer questions about unknown words in a text.

Reinforce the use of questions to help students determine the meanings of unknown words in the text. As you set a purpose for reading in the EXPLORE section, point out the bold words *blizzard* and *hurricane*. Remind students that the bold black type indicates that these are important words to know. Guide students in asking questions that can help them find the word's meanings. For example, point out the word *is* in each sentence where the bold terms appear. Explain that this word is a clue that a definition may follow. Say: **I might ask myself, "Where is the word *is* on the page? Is it in the same sentence as the boldfaced terms?"** Guide students to find this word and the definitions that follow.

Predicting Weather

NEXT GENERATION SCIENCE STANDARDS | DISCIPLINARY CORE IDEAS

ESS3.B: Natural Hazards Weather scientists forecast severe weather so that the communities can prepare for and respond to these events. (K-ESS3-2)

ETS1.A: Defining and Delimiting an Engineering Problem Asking questions, making observations, and gathering information are helpful in thinking about problems. (K–2-ETS1-1, *secondary to K-ESS3-2*)

NEXT GENERATION SCIENCE STANDARDS | PERFORMANCE EXPECTATION

K-ESS3-2. Ask questions to obtain information about the purpose of weather forecasting to prepare for, and respond to, severe weather. [Clarification Statement: Emphasis is on local forms of severe weather.]

K–2-ETS1-1. Ask questions, make observations, and gather information about a situation people want to change to define a simple problem that can be solved through the development of a new or improved object or tool.

Objective Students will be able to:

- Ask questions about weather forecasts to find out how to solve the problem of staying safe from severe weather.

ENGAGE

Tap Prior Knowledge

- Write the word *predict* on the board. Explain that *predict* means "to say that something might happen in the future."
- Ask: **When you look at the sun in a clear, blue sky, what might you predict about the weather that day?** (Possible answer: The weather will probably be clear and sunny.)
- Ask: **What other clues in nature could be used to predict the weather?** (Possible answers: Dark clouds might mean rain is coming. White fluffy clouds might mean nice weather. Cold temperatures and dark clouds might mean snow is coming.

EXPLORE

Preview the Lesson

- Read aloud the lesson's main heading. Then have students observe the large background picture on pages 28–29. Ask: **What does this picture show?** (Possible answers: It shows a lot of television screens. It shows a weather room. It shows maps and clouds on televisions. It shows someone looking at the maps and clouds.)
- Ask: **Where have you seen a room like this?** (Possible answer: I saw one on a news channel on television.)

Set a Purpose and Read

- Have students listen to find out about how weather predictions can help them stay safe.
- Have students follow along as you read pages 28–29.

EXPLAIN

Explain How Weather Forecasting Helps People

- After reading pages 28–29, ask: **What do you think scientists look at and think about when they study the weather?** (Possible answers: They look at the clouds. They look at maps to see where storms are. They look at how much rain or snow falls. They study the wind patterns.)
- Ask: **If a weather forecaster predicts rain in the afternoon, what questions could you ask to prepare for the rain?** (Possible answers: When will the rain start? How long will it rain? Will it rain hard or just drizzle? Should I wear my raincoat?) Ask: **If a weather forecaster predicts a hot sunny day, what questions could you ask to prepare for the heat?** (Possible answers: Will it be warm enough to wear shorts? Will it be hot enough to go swimming?)

Explain How Weather Forecasting Helps Communities

- Display the picture of a blizzard on page 25. Say: **Suppose forecasters predict a blizzard.** Ask: **What questions could you ask to help you stay safe?** (Possible answers: Should I go

SCIENCE AND ENGINEERING PRACTICES

Asking Questions and Defining Problems

- In this lesson students discovered that scientists ask questions about weather conditions to help them predict if bad weather will cause problems in the near future. Ask: **How do you think scientists who study weather ask questions and make observations to help you?** (They make observations ask questions about what will likely happen. They help warn me when bad weather is coming.)
- Discuss with students how people have come up with ways to protect them from the weather. For Example rainstorms can make people wet. People have designed solutions to this problem. Ask: **What are some ways people stay dry when it is raining.** (possible answer: They use umbrellas. They use bus shelters. They wear waterproof jackets.)

Obtaining, Evaluating, and Communicating Information

- Ask: **How can you use media to obtain information about weather patterns?** (I can watch the weather on the news or check on the computer to see if bad weather is expected.)

CROSSCUTTING CONCEPTS

Cause and Effect

- Discuss with students how changes in the weather have a cause and effect. For example dark clouds in the sky can lead to rain. Ask students if they can think of any other example of cause and effect from their science lessons. For example pushing or pulling on an object can change its direction.

Connections to Engineering, Technology, and Applications of Science
Interdependence of Science, Engineering, and Technology

- People encounter questions about the natural world every day. Discuss with students the kind of questions they would like to answer that apply to science and weather. Record their questions on the board.

Influence of Engineering, Technology, and Science on Society and the Natural World

- Discuss how people depend on various technologies in their lives; human life would be very different without technology. Ask: **How do you depend on technology to answer your questions as they relate to weather?** (Possible answers: I watch tv or use a computer or smartphone to see if the weather person has observed patterns to let me know what the weather will be like.)

EXPLAIN

to school today? How can I dress warmly enough to stay safe?)

- Say: **Sometimes forecasters see a pattern that tells them a tornado is possible or is moving toward a certain location. Then people in charge of your community will make announcements on television and radio. They will send alerts to adults' cell phones. The announcements will tell people to take shelter.**
- Revisit the picture of a hurricane on page 27. Say: **Suppose forecasters predict a hurricane.** Ask: **What questions could you ask to help you stay safe?** (Possible answer: Should we leave our house for a safer place?)
- Say: **If forecasters predict a very strong hurricane, people in charge of your community will announce that you should leave your home and go to a safer place. They will tell you where safer places are. After the storm, they will tell you when it is safe to return to your house.**

ELABORATE

Find Out More About Weather Forecasting

My science notebook

Help students find out more about weather forecasting. Read students a weather book for children, such as *Freddy the Frogcaster*, or *Freddy the Frogcaster and the Big Blizzard* by meteorologist Janice Dean. Students will explore weather forecasting in the context of a fun story written for their age level. You can download a weather journal from a book-related website and have students use the journal to forecast local weather.

Extend Your Thinking About Local Weather Forecasting

My science notebook Show students how to access a local daily weather forecast created just for young children. You can find the "Weather Report for Kids" on the Internet. By typing in your zip code, you can get today's weather as well as tomorrow's forecast for your local area. Pictures show the weather and suggest appropriate attire for that weather.

EVALUATE

My science notebook Have students record the answer to the Wrap It Up question in their science notebook.

Wrap It Up!

1. ANALYZE **What questions can you ask to help you stay safe?** (Answers will vary. Students may ask questions such as: Where should I go during a storm? What should I do to protect myself? Where can I get information about the storm?)

NATIONAL GEOGRAPHIC LEARNING | Science Career

Weather Expert

NEXT GENERATION SCIENCE STANDARDS | CONNECTIONS TO NATURE OF SCIENCE
Scientific Knowledge Is Based on Empirical Evidence Scientists look for patterns and order when making observations about the world.

Objective Students will be able to:
- Connect weather patterns with the career of a weather expert.

ENGAGE

Tap Prior Knowledge

- Have students who have seen a weather report on television describe what the weather experts do. Ask probing questions to encourage exploration. For example, ask: **What other jobs do you think weather experts might do? What tools do you think they use to study the weather?** Use students' ideas as a starting point for guiding them to understand what weather experts do.

EXPLORE

Preview the Lesson

- Have students look at the weather expert on page 30. Say: **This woman's name is Sepi Yalda. She's a weather expert, but she's not on television. She has a different kind of weather career.**

Set a Purpose and Read

- Have students listen to connect weather patterns to the career of a weather expert.
- Have students follow along as you read page 30.

EXPLAIN

Describe How Sepi Yalda Became a Weather Expert

- Read aloud the first two sentences on page 30. Ask: **Why did Sepi Yalda decide to become a weather expert?** (She liked science in school. She was interested in weather.) Ask: **What did Sepi study in college?** (She studied weather.) Ask: **What work does Sepi do?** (She tries to make better tools for predicting the weather.)

Connect Weather Patterns to a Weather Expert Career

- Display the *Weather Patterns* lesson on pages 20–21. Point out the sunny weather and rainy weather in the same place. Say: **You learned that weather has patterns. Weather changes over time.**
- Ask: **How have we made observations about the weather?** (We used our eyes to observe clouds and sun. We decided how the air felt [warm or cool] on our skin. We observed whether it was raining.) **What did we do with our observations?** (We looked for patterns.) **What patterns did we see?** (Answers will vary with weather observed by students.) Say: **Sepi Yalda studies weather patterns. She thinks about the tools weather experts use. Then she tries to make better tools.**

Find Out More

- Ask: **Is this a career you would find interesting? Why or why not?** (Answers will vary. Accept all positive and negative responses.) For students who find this to be an interesting career, ask: **Why would you like to be a weather expert?** (Possible answer: I would like to be a weather expert because I'm interested in the weather.)

ELABORATE

Find Out More About What Weather Experts Do

My science notebook Project pictures or videos from the Internet of a variety of weather-related careers. For example, show a storm chaser with equipment on a truck; an incident meteorologist at a wildfire reporting wind speed and direction to the firefighting team; and a hurricane hunter who flies a plane into the eye of a hurricane to gather data. Ask probing questions to encourage explorations. For example, ask:

- **What are these people doing?**
- **Where do they work?**
- **What tools do they use?**
- **What role do computers play in being a weather expert?**

Have students tell which weather career interests them the most and explain why.

EVALUATE

My science notebook Ask students these questions. Have them record the answers in their science notebook.

1. EXPLAIN **How did Sepi Yalda's education prepare her for her career?** (She liked science and weather. She studied weather in college.)
2. PREDICT **How might better tools help forecasters keep people safe?** (Possible answer: Better tools might lead to better forecasts. These might help people stay safe from severe weather.)

ELL SUPPORT

Describe a Weather Expert Career

Beginning Ask yes/no questions, such as: **Are all weather careers the same?** (No.) **Is Sepi Yalda a weather expert?** (Yes.)

Intermediate Provide sentence frames, such as: *Sepi studied (weather) in college. Now Sepi makes (better tools) for predicting weather.*

Advanced Help students complete sentence stems that describe Sepi Yalda's work. Provide these stems: *When Sepi was in school, she … In college, Sepi … Sepi's job is …*

READING CONNECTION

Retell Key Details

With prompting and support, ask and answer questions about key details in a text.

Guide students to ask and answer questions as they read to help them identify and understand key details in the text. For example, in the ENGAGE section before you set a purpose for reading, point out and read the main heading, *Weather Expert*. Challenge students to think of questions they have about the career of weather expert. Have students listen for the answers to their questions as you read. Then in the EXPLAIN section have students discuss how the details in the text helped them answer their questions.

Test Administration Script for DCI Review: Earth Science

For Questions 1–10

SAY: You are going to take a short test about weather. Listen to the directions. (Hold up a page and point.) For each question, you will look at the pictures and listen to a question. Then you will circle one picture to mark your answer. Before you start, are there any questions? (Pause.)

1. Find number 1. Circle the picture that shows sunlight warming Earth. (PS3.B)
2. Find number 2. Circle the picture that shows one kind of weather. (ESS2.D)
3. Find number 3. Circle the picture that shows cloudy weather. (ESS2.D)
4. Find number 4. Circle the picture that shows windy weather. (ESS2.D)
5. Find number 5. Circle the picture that shows a rainy day. (ESS2.D)
6. Find number 6. Look at the picture on the right of the sunny day. Circle the picture that shows a change in the weather pattern. (ESS2.D)
7. Find number 7. Look at the picture on the right of the cloudy day. Circle the picture that shows the same weather pattern. (ESS2.D)
8. Find number 8. Circle the picture that shows a tornado. (ESS3.B)
9. Find number 9. Circle the picture that shows a blizzard. (ESS3.B)
10. Find number 10. Circle the picture that shows a weather expert predicting weather. (ESS3.B)

Name ______________________________

DCI Review: Earth Science

1

A

B

C

2

A

B

C

3

A

B

C

4

A

B

C

Name ______________________

5

A

B

C

6

A

B

Name ____________________

7

A

B

8

A

B

C

Name ______________________ Date __________

9

A

B

C

10

A

B

C

Pauta para tomar la prueba para el repaso de las IDB: Ciencias de la Tierra

Para las preguntas 1 a 10

DIGA: Van a dar una prueba corta sobre el tiempo. Escuchen las instrucciones. (Muestre una página y señálela). Para cada pregunta, mirarán los dibujos y escucharán una pregunta. Luego, encerrarán su respuesta en un círculo. Antes de comenzar, ¿tienen alguna duda? (Haga una pausa).

1. Hallen el número 1. Encierren en un círculo el dibujo que muestra que la luz solar calienta la Tierra. (PS3.B)

2. Hallen el número 2. Encierren en un círculo el dibujo que muestra un tipo de tiempo. (ESS2.D)

3. Hallen el número 3. Encierren en un círculo el dibujo que muestra el tiempo nublado. (ESS2.D)

4. Hallen el número 4. Encierren en un círculo el dibujo que muestra el tiempo ventoso. (ESS2.D)

5. Hallen el número 5. Encierren en un círculo el dibujo que muestra un día lluvioso. (ESS2.D)

6. Hallen el número 6. Observen el dibujo a la derecha del día soleado. Encierren en un círculo el dibujo que muestra un cambio en el patrón del tiempo. (ESS2.D)

7. Hallen el número 7. Observen el dibujo a la derecha del día nublado. Encierren en un círculo el dibujo que muestra el mismo patrón del tiempo. (ESS2.D)

8. Hallen el número 8. Encierren en un círculo el dibujo que muestra un tornado. (ESS3.B)

9. Hallen el número 9. Encierren en un círculo el dibujo que muestra una ventisca. (ESS3.B)

10. Hallen el número 10. Encierren en un círculo el dibujo que muestra a un experto en el tiempo prediciendo el tiempo. (ESS3.B)

Nombre ____

Repaso de las IDB: Ciencias de la Tierra

1

A

B

C

2

A

B

C

3

A

B

C

4

A

B

C

Nombre ______________________________

5

A

B

C

6

A

B

Nombre ______________________________

7

A

B

8

A

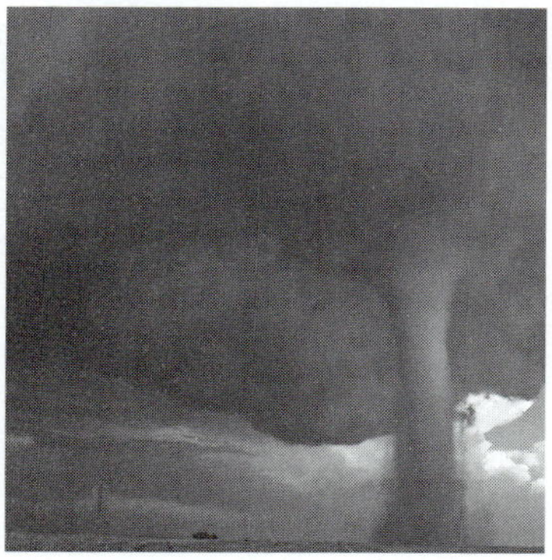

B

C

Nombre ____________________

9

A

B

C

10

A

B

C

DCI Review Answer Key for Earth Science

EARTH SCIENCE
K. Weather and Climate

Question Number	Answer
1	B
2	A
3	C
4	A
5	C
6	B
7	A
8	B
9	B
10	B

Name ______________________________ Date ____________________

Investigate

Weather

Question How does the weather change from morning to afternoon?

Directions Do you need a jacket? Color or circle your answer.

	Morning		Afternoon	
	Jacket	No Jacket	Jacket	No Jacket
Monday				
Tuesday				
Wednesday				
Thursday				
Friday				

Nombre ______________________ Fecha ______________

My science notebook

Investigación

Tiempo

Pregunta ¿Cómo cambia el tiempo de la mañana a la tarde?

Instrucciones ¿Necesitas chaqueta? Colorea o encierra tu respuesta en un círculo.

	Mañana		Tarde	
	Chaqueta	Sin chaqueta	Chaqueta	Sin chaqueta
Lunes				
Martes				
Miércoles				
Jueves				
Viernes				

Name ______________________________ Date ____________________

Investigate

Weather Patterns

Question How does weather change from day to day?

Directions Record the weather each day.

	Temperature 	Clouds 	Wind 	Rain 
Monday				
Tuesday				
Wednesday				
Thursday				
Friday				

Nombre ______________________ Fecha ______________

Investigación

Patrones del tiempo

Pregunta ¿Cómo cambia el tiempo de un día a otro?

Instrucciones Anota cómo está el tiempo todos los días.

	Temperatura 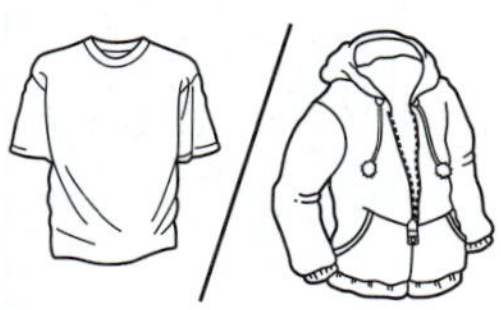	Nubes 	Viento 	Lluvia 
Lunes				
Martes				
Miércoles				
Jueves				
Viernes				

Program Authors

Randy L. Bell, Ph.D.
Associate Dean and Professor of Science Education, College of Education, Oregon State University

Malcolm B. Butler, Ph.D.
Associate Professor of Science Education, School of Teaching, Learning and Leadership, University of Central Florida

Kathy Cabe Trundle, Ph.D.
Department Head and Professor, STEM Education, North Carolina State University

Judith S. Lederman, Ph.D.
Associate Professor and Director of Teacher Education, Illinois Institute of Technology

Program Consultants

Gina Cervetti, Ph.D.
Assistant Professor of Literacy, Language, and Culture, University of Michigan

Nell K. Duke, Ed.D.
Professor of Literacy, Language, and Culture, University of Michigan

Philip E. Molebash, Ph.D.
Executive Director of the Center for Math and Science Teaching and Associate Professor, School of Education, Loyola Marymount University

---

Acknowledgments
Grateful acknowledgment is given to the authors, artists, photographers, museums, publishers, and agents for permission to reprint copyrighted material. Every effort has been made to secure the appropriate permission. If any omissions have been made or if corrections are required, please contact the Publisher.

Credits
Physical Science
P33 (tl) ©studio9400/iStockphoto.com. (tc) ©billyfoto/iStockphoto.com. (tr) ©Image Source/Alamy. (tcl) ©Photodisc/Getty Images. (tcc) ©Tetra Images/Alamy. (tcr) ©ShaneKato/iStockphoto.com. (bcl) ©Benis Arapovic/Shutterstock.com. (bcc) ©Corbis Super RF/Alamy. (bcr) ©Wave Royalty Free/Design Pics Inc/Alamy. (bl) ©LTuray/iStockphoto.com. (bc) ©RBFried/iStockphoto.com. (br) ©Dina Magnat/Shutterstock.com. **P34** (tl) ©hept27/iStockphoto.com. (tc) ©Image100/Jupiter Images. (tr) ©David Papazian/Stockbyte/Getty Images/Jupiter Images. (cl) ©darkscott/iStockphoto.com. (c) ©Suemack/iStockphoto.com. (cr) ©ShaneKato/iStockphoto.com. (bl) ©greenland/Shutterstock.com. (bc) ©John Lund/Tiffany Schoepp/Getty Images. (br) ©billyfoto/iStockphoto.com. **P35** (tl) ©Photodisc/Alamy. (tc) ©Shawn Pecor/Shutterstock.com. (tr) ©Nancy Honeycutt/iStockphoto.com. (cl) ©iStockphoto.com. (c) ©Digital Vision/Alamy. (cr) ©arabianEye FZ LLC/Alamy. (bl) ©John Foxx Images/Imagestate. (bc) ©Melanie DeFazio/Shutterstock.com. (br) ©JJ pixs/Alamy.

Life Science
L33 (tl) ©Heather G Delaney/Alamy. (tc) ©MetaTools. (tr) ©Kojihirano/Shutterstock.com. (tcl) ©Madlen/Shutterstock.com. (tcc) ©Kuttelvaserova Stuchelova/Shutterstock.com. (tcr) ©Stockbyte/Getty Images. (bcl) ©Hydromet/shutterstock.com. (bcc) ©photohoo/iStockphoto.com. (bcr) ©Creatas/Jupiterimages. (bc) ©John Foxx Images/Imagestate. (bl) ©Ian McDonnell/iStockphoto.com. (br) ©PhotoDisc/Getty Images. **L34** (tc) ©drisley77/iStockphoto.com. (tl) ©awc007/iStockphoto.com. (tr) ©tepic/iStockphoto.com. (cl) ©vovan/Shutterstock.com. (cr) ©Africa Studio/Shutterstock.com. (c) ©Kasiam/iStockphoto.com. (bl) ©EuroStyle Graphics/Alamy. (bc) ©marilyn barbone/Shutterstock.com. (br) ©Craig Hosterman/Shutterstock.com. **L35** (tl) ©J. Norman Reid/Shutterstock.com. (tc) Leonard Lee Rue III/Photo Researchers/Getty Images. (tr) ©Geostock/Photodisc/Getty Images. (cl) ©drisley77/iStockphoto.com. (c) ©Alan Ward/Shutterstock.com. (cr) ©Arnold John Labrentz/Shutterstock.com. (bl) ©Digital Vision/Getty Images. (bc) ©diane39/iStockphoto.com. (br) ©Kitch Bain/Shutterstock.com.

Earth Science
E33 (tr) ©Cheryl Casey/Shutterstock.com. (tc) ©Enjoylife2/iStockphoto.com. (tl) ©JennaWagner/iStockphoto.com. (tcl) ©Dainis Derics/Shutterstock.com. (tcr) ©laartist/iStockphoto.com. (tcc) ©PhotoDisc/Getty Images. (bcl) ©Creatas/age footstock. (bcc) ©David Hughes/Shutterstock.com. (bcr) ©PhotoDisc/Getty Images. (bl) ©Jim Lopes/Shutterstock.com. (bc) ©Saurabh/Flickr Open/Getty Images. (br) ©Mike Flippo/Shutterstock.com. **E34** (tl) ©Perry Correll/Shutterstock.com. (tc) ©Mark Yuill/Shutterstock.com. (tr) ©Jorge Salcedo/Shutterstock.com. (bl) ©iStockphoto.com. (cr) ©Stockbyte/Getty Images. (br) ©Dainis Derics/Shutterstock.com. **E35** (tr) ©Matthias Scholz/Alamy. (tl) ©John Foxx Images/Imagestate. (cr) ©Cheryl Casey/Shutterstock.com. (bl) ©Joel Sartore/National Geographic Creative. (bc) ©Willoughby Owen/Flickr RF/Getty Images. (br) ©Creatas/Jupiterimages. **E36** (tl) ©natureslight/Alamy. (tc) ©Gabe Palmer/The Image Bank/Getty Images. (tr) ©Fotofeeling/Alloy/Corbis. (bl) ©Sportstock/iStockphoto.com. (bc) ©AP Images/Alan Diaz. (br) ©Borge Ousland/National Geographic Creative.

Visit National Geographic Learning online at NGL.Cengage.com

Visit our corporate website at www.cengage.com

Printed in the USA.

Quad Graphics
Taunton, MA

ISBN: 978-13051-09971

18 19 20 21 22 23 24

10 9 8 7 6 5

NOTES